Contents

About the Author iv

Acknowledgments v

Preface vi

Chapter 1: The Unique Nature of Associations 2

Chapter 2: Governance Structures and Volunteer Roles 12

Chapter 3: Staff Structure and Roles 24

Chapter 4: Volunteer Management 30

Chapter 5: Budgeting and Finance. 38

Chapter 6: Marketing Basics 46

Chapter 7: Membership 54

Chapter 8: Publishing 64

Chapter 9: Education and Meetings 72

Chapter 10: Voluntary Standards 80

Chapter 11: Research and Statistics. 88

Chapter 12: Suppliers as a Market 92

Chapter 13: Government Relations 100

Chapter 14: The Public 108

Chapter 15: Foundations and Fund Raising 116

Chapter 16: Strategic Planning. 122

Chapter 17: Trends Forecasting 130

Related Resources 135

About the Author

As president of Ernstthal & Associates, Washington, D.C., **Henry L. Ernstthal, CAE**, is a speaker and consultant on such diverse topics as association governance and corporate structure, board orientation, committee and board productivity, contemporary legal issues, ethics and ethical behavior, forecasting and the future, managing computerization, managing for consensus, and strategic planning.

From 1989 to 1995, he was the only full-time faculty of the Master of Association Management degree program at The George Washington University. Before that, Ernstthal served 10 years as executive director of the Society of Nuclear Medicine, an 11,000-member international medical and scientific society, and as executive director of the California Dental Association.

A past president of the New York Society of Association Executives and a past vice chairman of the American Society of Association Executives (ASAE), Ernstthal was named an ASAE Fellow in 1988. He holds a B.A. from Wesleyan University in Middletown, Connecticut, and a J.D. from Stanford Law School.

Acknowledgments

In preparing this fourth edition, my greatest debt is to Bob Jones IV who provided much of the polish and many of the sidebars in the third edition which continue to be relevant in the fourth. I'm also grateful to several ASAE Fellows who took the time to read some of the chapters and make suggestions and recommendations for their improvement. They are: Janet McCallen, CAE; Paul Pomerantz, CAE; Betsy Kovacs, CAE; Lee VanBremen, Ph.D., CAE; Michael Gallery, Ph.D., CAE; and Sherry Keramidas, Ph.D., CAE.

I also appreciate the efforts of Linda Munday, Anna Nunan, and Louise Quinn of the ASAE staff for all their help on this book. Sandy Sabo, editor of the book, smoothed out the rough spots and tolerated my last-minute delays above and beyond the call of duty.

My wife, Mary Lynn Ernstthal, an association executive, provided her usual generous and unfailing support.

Henry L. Ernstthal, CAE

Preface

Perhaps you are thinking about taking an association job for the first time or have recently accepted one in which to get up to speed. Or maybe you've been in the association sector for some time and simply want to brush up on the basics or prepare for the Certified Association Executive (CAE) exam. Whatever your situation, this fourth edition of *Principles of Association Management* is intended to be both useful and interesting for a diverse audience.

This fourth edition includes updated information from the latest ASAE studies. In the third edition, one chapter addressed the future of association management. In some significant ways, particularly in the area of technology, the content of that chapter was outstripped by events in short order. Replacing that chapter in the fourth edition, "Trends Forecasting" addresses techniques that association executives can use to help identify and assess the future trends that will effect their organization's future.

Writing a book directed at both the newcomer and the seasoned pro is no small task. Because the guiding principle has been to assume little or no prior knowledge on the part of the reader, I have tried to explain terms and expunged jargon whenever possible. To give beginners a frame of reference, the book also attempts to give concrete examples that illustrate or illuminate abstract principles and theories. More experienced readers will find some thought-provoking concepts and sophisticated ideas presented, I trust, in deceptively simple language.

Because no book can possibly say everything possible about association management, you will also find a list of Related Resources after Chapter 17.

Henry L. Ernstthal, CAE

Principles of Association Management

Fourth Edition

by
Henry L. Ernstthal, CAE

Washington, DC

Information in this book is accurate as of the time of publication and consistent with standards of good practice in the general management community. As research and practice advance, however, standards may change. For this reason, it is recommended that readers evaluate the applicability of any recommendation in light of particular situations and changing standards.

American Society of Association Executives
1575 I Street, NW
Washington, DC   20005-1103
Phone: (202) 626-2723
Fax: (202) 408-9634
E-mail: books@asaenet.org
ASAE's core purpose is to advance the value of voluntary associations to society and to support the professionalism of the individuals who lead them.
Susan Robertson, Vice President, Marketing & Communications
Anna Nunan, Director of Book Publishing
Louise Quinn, Acquisitions Coordinator
Jennifer Moon, Production Manager
Anthony Conley, Operations Coordinator

Cover design by Design Consultants, interior design by Black Dot Group

This book is available at a special discount when ordered in bulk quantities. For information, contact the ASAE Member Service Center at (202) 371-0940.

A complete catalog of titles is available on the ASAE Web site at www.asaenet.org/bookstore

Library of Congress Cataloging-in-Publication Data
Ernstthal, Henry L.
    Principles of association management / by Henry L. Ernstthal.—4th ed.
        p. cm.
    Includes bibliographical references and index.
    ISBN 0-88034-175-0
    1. Trade associations—United States—Management. I. Jones, Bob, IV. II. American Society of Association Executives. III. Title.

HD2421 .P7 2001
060'.68—dc21   2001022126

Printed in the United States of America.

10   9   8   7   6   5   4   3

The Unique Nature of Associations

Key Points

- Trade associations have companies or businesses as members, while professional societies and affinity groups have individuals as members. Federations have associations as members.

- The United States has more than 23,000 national; more than 116,000 state, local, and regional; and 1,300 international associations.

- The uniqueness of associations rests in their members' strong feelings of ownership and involvement in decision making. Members believe they can make themselves heard and effect change within and through their associations.

No other country has an association sector as active and fully developed as the United States. Boasting more than 23,000 national associations at the opening of the 21st century, the United States has institutionalized an impulse that dates back thousands of years. In fact, recent studies of evolutionary psychology argue that the instinct for cooperation constituted an evolutionary advantage and is part of our genetic structure.

The Book of Genesis mentions that members of the same trade or craft tended to congregate geographically. Historians believe that associations existed in ancient Egypt and China, and in Roman times the trades maintained apprentice training agreements and protective regulations. The ancient Phoenician merchants who plied the seas also often banded together to form mutual-aid societies.

These groups undoubtedly bore little resemblance to today's multifaceted trade associations and professional societies. But by the 16th century, organizations had begun to emerge that could be easily recognized as "true" associations. Throughout much of western Europe, merchants and artisans joined together in powerful guilds that governed production, monitored sales, maintained apprentice training programs, oversaw wages and hours, and inspected finished products.

Trade Associations in America

Although guilds existed during the colonial period, they had long passed their zenith of power. In fact, the American public had come to view guilds negatively, thanks to practices such as price fixing, regulation, and suppression of the entrepreneurial spirit. On the other hand, the spirit of cooperative effort characterized the dispersion of the population across the continent. The cooperation of farmers in their communities, the establishment of schools and churches, and the formation of local governments were all evidence of the young country's voluntary spirit.

As guilds slowly disappeared, other kinds of trade associations arose to take their place. For example, 20 merchants founded the Chamber of Commerce of the State of New York in 1768, and it continues to thrive. Its closest competitor for bragging rights as "oldest continuing association" is the New York Stock Exchange, established in 1792.

The formation of trade associations—in which companies or businesses hold memberships—continued at a languid pace through the early years of the republic. A spurt of activity occurred during the Civil War years as both the North and the South organized efforts to make the best use of their industrial assets. The period of Reconstruction (1865–1877) that followed saw unprecedented industrial expansion, especially in the railroads; trade associations grew accordingly, reaching about 100 in number.

According to the National Industrial Conference Board, "trade associations began to assume the dignity of definite business institutions" by 1890. In other words, the associations maintained offices, elected officials, and held regular meetings. Although they may have served largely a social function in the latter part of the 19th century, trade associations also lobbied Congress and state legislatures and carried out programs such as quality inspection, standardization, and credit improvement.

About this time, however, trade associations began to exhibit some of the negative aspects of the guilds they had replaced. Monopoly was a common goal among business owners, and their associations engaged in price fixing, production controls, territorial allocation, and distribution management. At the time, American business viewed over supply as a constant threat and favored cooperation among producers as the key to ensuring profits. During the late 19th century, the word "cooperation" would have been defined as limiting the available supply, maintaining a fixed price regardless of demand, and granting exclusivity for distribution of products in geographic territories.

To curb such abuses, Congress passed the Sherman Antitrust Act in 1890. In a series of cases interpreting the act, the U.S. Supreme Court found that information exchanges could further the public interest. The court held that an association could provide price information—but only on past transactions—and that its members could make no agreements to maintain prices based on such information. Furthermore, associations had to make the statistics they'd gathered available to nonmembers, banks, and the U.S. Department of Commerce.

When World War I began in 1914, the United States probably had 1,000 trade associations. By 1920, thanks to industry's rapid mobilization for war and the need for quick, voluntary coordination, the count had doubled to 2,000 (of these, 600 were national in scope). Commenting on this period, War Production Board Chairman Bernard Baruch later said, "Many businessmen experienced during the war, for the first time in their careers, the tremendous advantages both to themselves and to the general public, of combination, of cooperation, and common action with their natural competitors."

Associations became more professional in the ensuing years, hiring staff members and establishing their own professional society. (The American Trade Association Executives, the precursor to the American Society of Association Executives, was founded in 1920.) Some of the New Deal agencies created during the 1930s, such as the National Recovery Administration, required full-time staff to handle the increasing interaction between business and government.

By the time the United States entered World War II in 1941, associations could contribute significantly to the war effort on the homefront. During the first few weeks of the war, for instance, the Association of American Railroads coordinated the movement of some 600,000 troops. The Council of Machine Tool and Equipment Services indexed suppliers of machinery and parts, enabling defense contractors to quickly locate urgently needed items. Associations also provided technical specialists to government departments, took part in conservation campaigns, and provided a vital link between the government and individual companies.

Development of Professional Societies

Professional societies can trace their roots back to the late Renaissance, when scientific societies were formed to collect and disseminate knowledge. The earliest of these societies, the Academia Secretorum Naturae of Naples, was organized in 1560.

The philosophy of Enlightenment that flowered during the 18th century provided the key to the growth of professional societies, in which individuals hold membership. As the division of labor became more pronounced and scholars became more revered, educated people could spend more time delving deeply into their particular field of specialization. They systematically organized and recorded the bodies of knowledge of various occupations for the benefit of future generations. Professionalism in the modern sense had begun to develop.

In the United States, professional societies got a 100-year jump on their counterparts in the trades: Benjamin Franklin founded the American Philosophical Society in Philadelphia in 1743, making it the oldest American scientific society still in existence. Another venerable society, the American Academy of Arts and Sciences (AAAS), got its start in 1780 in Boston. AAAS proved the exception, however. The practical considerations of establishing a new nation so consumed learned men and women that few national professional societies developed in the years after the American Revolution.

The 1840s brought a short spurt of activity, including the founding of the American Statistical Association (1839), the American Psychiatric Association

(1844), and the American Medical Association (1847). Following a hiatus during the Civil War years, professional and scientific societies resumed their growth as urbanization and industrialization provided a fertile breeding ground for new specialties and expanding bodies of knowledge. Professional societies became the de facto guardians of this knowledge, disseminating new information, maintaining standards of professionalism, and serving as research consultants for governments and universities.

The diversity of associations makes it difficult to create a clear set of categories that have no overlap. In general, the term "professional societies" encompasses three types of organizations:

1. Scientific, engineering, or learned societies that strive to advance the body of knowledge in their fields. Such societies are as diverse as the National Council of Teachers of English, the American Society of Clinical Hypnosis, and the Association of Pediatric Oncology Nurses, all of which keep their members up to date on trends and developments in their respective areas.

2. Affinity groups that bring together people who share a common interest outside their area of employment. Examples include the American Philatelic Society and the American Contract Bridge League.

3. Religious, charitable, public service, or fraternal organizations that have a particular cause or belief as a rallying point. Again, the range is large and runs the gamut from the National Council on Aging to the American Lung Association to Delta Upsilon Fraternity.

Modern Associations

Taken together, trade associations and professional societies of all types constitute a pervasive force in American society. Almost everyone joins at least one voluntary association at some time, and hundreds of thousands make their living working in the association sector. Associations are the largest provider of adult education services in the United States and contribute some $100 billion to the economy each year.

NUTS ABOUT PROMOTION

Do associations really make a difference? Just consider the case of the pecan industry, which lacks a unified voice in the United States.

From Virginia to the Southwest, pecan trees can be found in huge commercial orchards as well as Main Street backyards. Some even grow wild in city parks. This abundance of trees means that almost anyone can be considered a pecan grower, even if their trees' annual output totals just a few pounds.

In the early 1990s, the Pecan Growers Board implemented a one-year plan to collect a half-cent contribution on every pound of unshelled pecans produced by growers of all sizes. The money was earmarked for research and education projects to develop new recipes, increase public awareness, and publicize nutritional information. At the end of the year, the producers would vote on whether to continue the program.

Smaller growers, who together account for about one-third of the total annual pecan crop, rebelled against the assessment. Because of a rule giving one vote to any grower producing at least one pound of pecans per year, the smaller growers overwhelmed their larger counterparts and rejected the plan.

That same year the Almond Board of California, Modesto, launched a media blitz, complete with free samples, seasonal recipes, and nutritional information. The association lined up a nutritionist to appear on radio talk shows and supplied media personnel with story ideas, glossy photos, and sample interview questions. Says one announcer who had a radio nutrition show at the time, "I used the stuff from the almond people a lot. They always had good information, and they were very professional to work with."

And the pecan people? She pauses, thinking hard. "I don't remember ever getting anything from them . . . ."

According to statistics gathered by the American Society of Association Executives (ASAE) in 2000:

- The United States has more than 23,000 national; more than 116,000 state, local, and regional; and 1,300 international associations.
- Nine out of ten adult Americans belong to one association; one out of four belongs to four or more associations.
- Associations employ approximately 295,000 people in the United States.

The Internal Revenue Service (IRS) classifies different types of not-for-profit organizations under Section 501(c) of the U.S. Tax Code. The majority of business-related organizations fall into the 501(c)(6) category, while some professional societies opt for 501(c)(3) status as a charitable organization and other groups for 501(c)(4) status as a social welfare organization. (Note: This book does not address labor unions, private foundations, hospitals, churches, or volunteer-based charitable organizations that provide direct human services.)

Outside the IRS codes, it's not always easy to draw distinctions between associations and charitable organizations. For example, should you categorize a cause- or health-related group, such as the American Heart Association or the American Cancer Society, as an association? Such organizations do much of their work at the local level and, like traditional charities, focus on activities such as direct-mail fund raising, development of major gifts, service delivery, and research support. But in their governance, where volunteers help make decisions on a wide range of specialized issues, these organizations are frequently more akin to (c)(6) associations than (c)(3) local charities.

Frequently, charitable organizations, like some associations, appear to be federations—national or international associations whose members are smaller associations with a common interest. For example, United Way of America comprises neither businesses nor individuals but rather local United Way affiliates. But the United Way's board of directors functions in typical association fashion, although its structure may be more diverse, with representation from major corporations as well as state and local United Way or Community Chest organizations.

Comparisons to Business

Comparing associations to businesses can clarify their roles and provide a better understanding of their unique nature. Here's how the two differ:

- Size. All but the very largest associations would be considered, at best, small businesses. In fact, only five of the 50 largest associations report revenues of more than $50 million, the generally accepted cut-off point for small businesses. Rarely do associations get past that point and enter the realm of the mid-sized business.

ASSOCIATIONS TODAY

National associations in the United States are classified as follows:

Trade, Business, and Commercial	4,005
Environmental and Agricultural	1,146
Legal, Governmental, Public Administration, and Military	395
Engineering, Technological, and Natural and Social Sciences	1,336
Educational	1,320
Cultural	1,920
Social Welfare	1,964
Health and Medical	2,512
Public Affairs	2,094
Fraternal, Nationality, and Ethnic	584
Religious	1,220
Veterans, Hereditary, and Patriotic	897
Hobby and Avocational	1,579
Athletic and Sports	825
Labor Unions, Associations, and Federations	250
Chambers of Commerce and Trade and Tourism	143
Greek and Non-Greek Letter Societies, Associations, and Federations	333
Fan Clubs	536

Source: Encyclopedia of Associations, 35th edition (1999).

- Mission. A business has a clear and defining purpose: profitability. An association's reason for being, however, might be conducting research, fostering public service, representing private interests to government, or educating the public—all of which are tax-exempt purposes.

- Structure. Businesses typically have a pyramid-shaped hierarchy that lends itself to an easy explanation of levels of authority, decision making, responsibility, and so forth.

  In associations, power is much more diffuse. Although their paid staff members may be organized along a typical (though flatter) organizational chart, associations also must contend with myriad volunteer governance structures. These may include a house of delegates, a board of directors or trustees, committees and subcommittees, councils, special interest groups, and so forth. As a result, the interaction among association staff and volunteers can become quite complex.

  To survive, both businesses and associations must consider the environment in which they operate and the trends that are likely to affect them in the future. But while businesses can concentrate on the nature of what they do, associations must balance both the future of the trade or profession they represent and the future of the organization itself.

- Markets. A for-profit business has no set limits when defining its customers. As products mature and markets evolve, businesses have both the incentive and the flexibility to follow wherever those changes may lead. As Kellogg's "Tony the Tiger" ad campaign shows, a cereal product that was successfully targeted to the "baby boomers" when they were children can now be retargeted to them as adults.

On the other hand, associations are strictly defined by their primary market—the individuals or the companies in a given field that pay membership dues in exchange for information and services. Associations may also provide goods and services to individuals and companies other than their members—but there's no question that members form their core market. The Masking Tape Manufacturers Association, for instance, could probably not metamorphose into the Tape, Disk, and Billboard Society, no matter how lucrative some of those areas may appear. Still, as members and their products and services evolve, associations must respond to change or slowly fade away.

Beginning in the late 1980s, in response to economic pressures, businesses, institutions, and individuals became more bottom-line driven. In addition to demanding that their associations become "more businesslike," members now are less amenable to dues increases and carefully evaluate the value of membership. This approach to membership pressures associations to keep dues low and seek other sources of revenue (nondues income).

EXPANDING MARKETS

Having a well-defined market doesn't necessarily mean that associations remain static or stay away from new ventures or new nonmember customers.

A case in point is the Building Owners and Managers Association (BOMA), Washington, D.C., which quickly prepared educational materials to help its members understand and comply with the complexities of the Americans with Disabilities Act of 1990. As news of the materials spread, BOMA discovered that other businesses and associations also wanted a handy guide to the legislation and successfully broadened its marketing campaign for the publication.

Another example of expanding beyond an association's traditional market comes from the Annapolis, Maryland-based U.S. Naval Institute, a group of people involved in the arcana and technicalities of shipping and ship construction. When the institute received an unknown author's fast-paced fiction manuscript that also exhibited a keen grasp of naval operations, it quickly determined that the book would appeal to more than just engineers and retired officers. The gamble to publish its first work of fiction paid off handsomely for the institute: *The Hunt for Red October* became a best-seller in 1984 and made author Tom Clancy a household name.

In response, just under one in five associations (17 percent) has created a wholly owned, for-profit subsidiary. Three considerations typically prompt this strategy. First, to the extent that the revenue-generating activities are unrelated to the association's underlying mission, a separate subsidiary can help protect the parent organization's tax-exempt status. Second, a for-profit subsidiary can permit a more businesslike decision-making structure and allow the association to quickly introduce a product or service into the marketplace. Third, the subsidiary may provide some protection from liability. Most often, subsidiaries engage in activities related to insurance/employee benefits, group purchasing, publishing, and financial services.

As their name implies, associations create a sense of belonging among practitioners of a profession or managers of an industry. But the uniqueness of associations really rests in their members' strong feelings of ownership and involvement in decision making. The people and corporations that call themselves members believe they can make themselves heard and effect change within and through their trade association or professional society.

As long as associations continue to engender a sense of belonging and feelings of ownership, they'll maintain their place in American society as examples of the power of volunteerism and the democratic process. This unique sector will also continue to provide challenges and opportunities for those who find themselves in management roles within it. ∎

Governance Structures and Volunteer Roles

Key Points

- Governance is the participation of volunteers in making decisions that are crucial to the operation and viability of an organization.

- Each association must strike the elusive balance between members' broad participation and involvement on the one hand and the ability to make timely decisions on the other.

- An association's chief staff executive directs its staff and operations, with feedback from volunteers. Elected or appointed leaders set direction and establish policies, with input from and advice of staff.

Governance, in the context of associations, is the partici-pation of volunteers in making decisions that are crucial to the viability of an organization. For almost all associations— whether trade, professional, or charitable—the main governance responsibility rests with a board of directors or board of trustees. Sometimes this governing body goes by other names, including board of governors, house of delegates, or constituent assembly. Typically an organization's bylaws describe its governance structure and how power is allocated within it.

Of course, corporations and educational institutions have similar governing bod-ies. What's different about trade associations and professional societies is the scope of volunteer decision making beyond the board level. Large numbers of volunteers take an active role in governance through committees, task forces, and other entities that help shape an association's long-term direction and short-term priorities. In a well-functioning association, this type of government "of the people, by the people, and for the people" would have made the Founding Fathers proud.

Structural Options

Associations may exhibit a wide range of governance structures depending on their size, resources, and type of activities. As in architecture, form should follow function in association governance. For instance, a trade association with a small number of members may give each one a seat on the board of directors, while a professional society with thousands of members will develop some form of rep-resentative government.

Many professional societies have a house of delegates that acts as the senior policy-making body. Usually made up of representatives from geographic or other subdivisions of the membership, the house may range in size from 100 to more than 1,000 members. The presiding officer may be either the chief elected officer or a separately selected speaker of the house. Typically, when an association has a large house of delegates (or other large decision-making body), it also has a small-er board or committee empowered to make interim decisions or fulfill specific managerial responsibilities.

A federation (an association that has other associations as its primary members) often has a board comprised entirely of delegates selected by local chapters to represent their interests. Other associations may have a board structure similar to a federation, elect all representatives "at large," or have a board that features a combination of chapter delegates and at-large members. If size permits, some organizations vote on crucial decisions at meetings that all members may attend. Boards of charitable organizations, particularly at the local level, tend to consist of individuals who can provide access to the resources and prestige of various groups within the community or contribute a specific expertise.

What works for one association doesn't necessarily work for another. Each must strike the elusive balance between broad participation and involvement on the one hand and the ability to make timely decisions on the other. It's also crucial to balance the need for local or special interest group members to feel "represented" and the need to recruit board members with specific talent and expertise.

A VARIETY OF CHOICES

To illustrate the diversity exhibited by association governance structures, here are descriptions of how four smaller associations operate:

American League of Lobbyists (Professional Society)

- Total members: 500.
- Board of Directors: 18 (6 officers plus 12 directors).
- Additional bodies: 6-member senior council advises board.
- Selection: Nominating committee brings complete slate to annual meeting for approval.
- Selection criteria: Board members are usually past committee chairs and exhibit interest in the issues of the association.
- Meetings: 10 times per year.
- Observation: "Our board is invaluable. Their biggest hands-on role is getting program speakers and setting our direction on lobbying reform. The worst thing we've faced is the occasional board member who just doesn't do anything. We've never had a case of professional staff being driven crazy by volunteers." —Former Executive Director

Envelope Manufacturers Association of America (Trade Association)

- Total members: 130.
- Board of Directors: 16 (including a 4-member executive committee).
- Additional bodies: None.
- Selection: Largest companies in the industry rotate on and off the board, serving 3-year terms. Smaller companies are elected to represent their geographic area.
- Selection criteria: Small-company representatives are selected based on service, longevity, and leadership. All board members must serve as committee chairs at least once before board service begins.

- Meetings: Twice a year.
- Observation: "The value of the board of directors is to ensure that the association stays focused on its strategic objectives, that financial resources remain adequate to support the association's programs, and that government relations initiatives are carefully considered in terms of the direction of both the association and the industry." —Maynard Benjamin, CAE, President

American Czech & Slovak Association (Affinity Group)

- Total members: 700.
- Board of Directors: 8.
- Additional bodies: None.
- Selection: Membership receives a consensus slate of candidates.
- Selection criteria: No formal requirements.
- Meetings: 4 times per year.
- Observation: The biggest board-related problem is "communication and commitment. It's difficult to find people who will commit the time necessary." —Former President

American Nurses Association (Federation)

- Total members: 53 state associations, including D.C., Guam, and Puerto Rico.
- Board of Directors: 15.
- Additional bodies: House of Delegates (the board of directors reports to this 615-member body); Constituent Assembly—made up of the president and executive director of each state association (this is an informal but influential advisory body).
- Selection: Elected by the House of Delegates.
- Meetings: 4 times per year, plus a monthly conference call.
- Observation: "Our board is very active. Professionals tend to get more involved in the governance of their associations than you would typically find in the trades." Despite the three-tiered governance structure, "We're still trying to find the best way to represent various size constituencies. There are some flaws in the federation model." —Karen Tucker, CAE, Governance Director

Potential Areas of Conflict

Because governance concerns the allocation of power, it can become a source of tension. Here are the main areas where such tension might develop.

SPECIAL INTEREST GROUPS

Often, as organizations become larger, subsets of the membership desire to form a special interest group or section to address their specific interests, such as an evolving technology in a trade association or a new specialty within a professional society. Once established, these special interest groups' need for resources and desire for autonomy may conflict with the priorities of the parent organization.

As an example, one (c)(3) organization had members from both the for-profit and nonprofit sectors. As the for-profit segment grew, those members expressed a desire to lobby freely. To avoid a spin-off organization forming, the parent association formed a subsidiary (c)(6) trade association to serve the for-profit members. Another organization headed off problems by revising its board structure; it gave more power to a subgroup that had developed a large trade show which provided a large portion of the association's revenues.

CHAPTERS

The distribution of power in a multiple-level organization—such as a national or state association with state or local chapters—has an added measure of complexity. The national organization, focused on large-scale issues and activities, a need for nondues revenue, and its need to effectively lobby Congress and regulatory agencies on behalf of all members, expects chapters to support and participate in national initiatives. Meanwhile, chapters have their own concerns about revenue, legislation, and regulation at the state or local level.

The national organization may wonder why chapters don't provide more support, while chapters may resent the constant pressure to participate in spite of limited local resources. Exacerbating this ongoing conflict in recent years has been the federal government's shift of significant power back to the states; this has increased the importance of lobbying at the state level at the same time that many statewide organizations have reached maturity in terms of size and staffing. Managing chapter relations has become a much more significant issue for national or parent organizations, with mechanisms for resolving differences and building positive relationships still being developed.

COMMITTEES

Committees generally are responsible for either designing and operating a project or recommending policy to the board. Tension between committees and boards usually involves issues of emotional commitment and autonomy, plus the desire of the committees for ratification by the more senior governance body.

When denying a request or voting down a committee's recommendation, a governing board must be careful to articulate the rationale for its decision. Otherwise, the committee members may take the rejection personally and become discouraged enough to cease any innovative activities.

BOARD-STAFF RELATIONSHIPS

An association's chief staff executive directs its staff and operations—with volunteer feedback—while elected or appointed leaders set direction and establish policies—with staff input and advice. Although those distinctions may sound clear-cut, the balance of power and allocation of duties between the board and the chief staff executive can lead to conflict and ineffectiveness—or they can serve as a source of energy and achievement.

The most influential issue in this relationship is the level of trust between the chief staff executive and the board, a trust based on a common set of expectations and well-defined roles. Rarely do board members develop and agree on their expectations as a result of discussion, debate, and consensus between the entire board and the chief staff executive. Instead, many associations find that expectations and roles remain unclear or vary from one board member to another.

This isn't surprising, because each board member's expectations of the "proper management relationship" with the chief staff executive are shaped by his or her business or professional life or by service on other boards. For instance, a board member who is an independent professional or small-business owner accustomed to having control will have very different expectations than the senior executive of a large business who has highly developed delegation skills.

CLEARING THE AIR

The confusion that often characterizes the board-staff relationship can be clarified with a diagnostic tool that points out the wide range of perceptions among board members. Used properly, this exercise precipitates open discussion and consensus building about the appropriate roles of the board and the chief staff executive.

1. Describe a continuum that ranges from 1 to 10, with 1 representing a totally staff-driven association and 10 being a totally volunteer-driven association. (Note: "volunteer" is defined as someone participating in leadership of the organization; it is not to be confused with "member driven." Because members are an association's primary market, the organization always should be market [member] driven.)

2. Ask each board member to select two whole numbers, one that describes where he or she thinks the organization currently falls within that 1-to-10 scale and one that describes where it should fall.

3. The results are then charted to display the range of opinion of where the association is now and where it wants to be and the direction and extent of change. Rarely do selections made by the board members cluster around a single number, which would demonstrate a common understanding of drivenness and agreement as to where they are now or where they ought to be. More frequently, the opinions of the board members are scattered along the continuum and indicate a lack of agreement about the direction of the change that needs to take place.

Where board members share a common background, it's relatively easy to develop a clear consensus regarding the roles and decision-making authority of the board and staff. If, on the other hand, board members come from a wide variety of business and professional backgrounds and have different levels of supervisory experience, the chief staff executive can find it difficult to understand what the board as a whole expects of him or her.

In the absence of agreement on the role of the chief staff executive, any action taken probably will disappoint part of the board. Some members will feel that the prerogative for that decision should have rested with them. Others will feel that the chief staff executive didn't go far enough in exercising the discretion, which they thought the board had clearly delegated. To avoid such contentious board-staff relationships, the board and the chief staff executive should discuss and clarify the nature of their roles and relationships whenever a significant change in the board's membership occurs or when a new chief staff executive is hired. The first meeting of the newly elected board members is also a good time to reiterate, reconfirm, or amend this agreement.

Who Does What?

Years ago, association executives used to ask one another, "Is your organization staff driven or volunteer driven?" They assumed that a simple answer would provide an understanding of how an organization operated.

Then, in the late 1980s, the Foundation of the American Society of Association Executives (ASAE) commissioned John Dunlop to study governance in a wide variety of trade associations, professional societies, and charities. The result, *Leading the Association: Striking the Right Balance Between Staff and Volunteers*, revealed that charities are more staff driven than trade associations, which, in turn, are more staff driven than professional societies.

The typical composition of the boards in those various types of organizations helps explain the study's results. Members of charity boards tend to come from a wide variety of business and professional backgrounds. Charities, particularly at the local level, may have a chief staff person who is primarily a care provider with recognized expertise (local mental health agencies, domestic violence centers, and free medical clinics are good examples). Board members, frequently recruited by the chief staff executive, recognize that their primary role is to help raise funds and forge links with the community. Their lack of common background and their deference to the chief staff executive as an expert in the field prompt them to delegate a considerable amount of authority to staff members.

Business executives who serve on the boards of trade associations typically have experience with and thrive on delegation. In addition, board members themselves frequently have been delegated the responsibility of representing their company on the association's board. This increases the likelihood that board members of trade associations will, in turn, delegate effectively to the staff.

In professional societies the emotional link to the profession is strong, and individuals rather than corporations make the decision to participate. Professional societies tend to attract members who have few, if any, subordinates reporting to them. Because these professionals are accustomed to a high degree of control in their own work environments, they usually expect similar control as leaders of an association.

In *Boards That Make a Difference,* a ground-breaking book now in its second edition, John Carver writes that boards are responsible for six actions:

1. Establishing goals for the organization to achieve. This entails defining the mission, describing who the organization is designed to serve, establishing the essential goods and services that it should provide, and determining the geographic focus of the organization (see Chapter 16 on Strategic Planning).

2. Establishing limitations on the means used to achieve the ends. Traditionally, says Carver, most boards tell staff, "Don't do anything until we tell you it's okay. Anything not expressly permitted is forbidden." Instead of attending to broad goals, association leaders get wrapped up in second-guessing staff behaviors and require staff to seek approval before taking any action.

Carver stands this approach on its head, arguing that the board should proscribe just two areas: behaviors considered unethical in dealing with people and decisions considered imprudent in managing the organization's resources. Given those limits, anything not expressly forbidden is permitted—the reverse of the traditional approach. In addition, a reasonable interpretation of the "ethical and prudent" parameters that support a staff decision must prevail in a dispute.

3. Hiring the chief staff executive. In addition, the board holds the chief staff executive accountable for achieving goals without falling afoul of the ethical or prudent limitations. This gives both significant authority and accountability to the chief staff executive, a position that may not be entirely comfortable.

Historically, association executives found solace in the fact that board members or other volunteer leaders had significant decision-making authority, which meant that ultimate responsibility didn't rest solely with them. Carver's approach leaves the executive wholly answerable for specific actions taken within the broad parameters established by the board.

4. Focusing on matters of policy. To Carver, this means that the board must ask whether a broader or underlying policy issue is more appropriate for debate than a vote on a specific resolution. For example, a board may be called on to support or oppose a piece of legislation. Carver argues that, rather than discuss the specific legislation, the board should look at the broad policy issues implicit within the legislation and decide what stance the association should take on those issues. This would permit staff to deal with subsequent legislation related to similar issues without requesting board action each time.

5. Acting only as a body, not as individual board members. Individuals don't have the power to direct the activities of staff: If they want something accomplished, they must take the matter to the full board. Otherwise, their input to the staff is advisory and must be consistent with existing board policy. This obviates the problem of chief elected leaders who believe that the organization is theirs to direct as they wish during their tenure. It helps them recognize that a more appropriate role is to take the organization where it wants to go.

6. Monitoring results. The board sets a schedule for this activity. At each board meeting, the chief staff executive has an obligation to report his or her compliance with the board policies.

Effective Committees

John Carver also writes about the nature and roles of volunteer committees, the vehicles through which much association work has been done traditionally.

An executive board or volunteer committee usually does an association's work before any staff member is hired. This pattern of active volunteer participation continues even when the organization matures and staff size increases, as evidenced by the many sets of association bylaws that contain lengthy and elaborate descriptions of committees and their responsibilities.

The common pattern is to have a formal structure for board appointment of committees, with staff generally held accountable for the performance of those committees. The problem is that staff members typically have no direct say in determining the committees' structure, membership, or tasks. In other words, staff has the accountability without the authority.

Given the growing difficulty associations are experiencing in recruiting members to serve on board-appointed committees, Carver advocates changing the costly and inefficient committee structure. He believes in two types:

1. Board-appointed committees—made up of board members and sometimes others—to develop broad policy alternatives.

2. Staff-appointed committees to help in the day-to-day work.

Because the board can act only as a unit, Carver says, it's not appropriate for committees to offer the board a single recommendation. Rather, each committee should present alternative recommendations for the board to debate and then act on. If the staff determines that a committee is needed to help in its work—either by acting in an advisory capacity, as a focus group, or as a group of workers charged with specific tasks to accomplish—then they are free to make the appointments and remain accountable for the committee's performance.

Until they can assess the efficacy of Carver's model, the majority of associations must learn to operate effectively with their existing committee structure. For many that has meant minimizing the number of standing, or ongoing, committees with multiyear terms and replacing them with ad hoc committees that are assembled for a specific purpose and disbanded when their work has been completed. Committees usually have between eight and fifteen members, though they can vary greatly in size, depending on the issue being addressed, the expertise needed, and the timetable for action.

Setting the Agenda

A meeting agenda can help focus the attention of boards and committees on their roles—no one likes to feel rushed about making a decision or overwhelmed by minutiae. In addition, the trust built up in a board-staff relationship can be destroyed when surprises crop up during board deliberations.

Two factors contribute to sustaining trust and operating efficiently: the logistics of disseminating information and the structure of the agenda itself.

As for logistics, committees should always have a clear understanding of their authority and of what they are to accomplish—along with sufficient and appropriate materials to help them analyze and evaluate the issues—before a meeting convenes. It's ideal to have these materials in members' hands the weekend before the meeting. Committee and board members tend to be overcommitted, so allowing them time to review and ponder the issues in advance eliminates a potential source of complaints.

Meetings tend to follow certain patterns, as evidenced by the traditional model for a board agenda:

I. Call to order and establishment of a quorum.

II. Approval of the agenda.

III. Officers' reports in order of protocol, with the chief elected officer first and the chief staff executive at the end of the list.

IV. Reports of committees in alphabetical order.

V. Reports of individuals with liaison responsibility, also in alphabetical order, based on the organization with which they interact.

VI. Old business.

VII. New business.

VIII. Setting the time for the next meeting and adjournment.

This format, adapted from *Roberts' Rules of Order*, is based on instructions written well over a century ago for the management of large assemblies. Unfortunately, this format could bury important action items at the end of the Zoology Liaison Committee's report. Board members could find themselves packing up and heading for the door just when a significant item comes up on the agenda—which might prompt a motion to refer to the next meeting or cynical suggestions that the staff and leadership left the item for last in an attempt to push through a vote just before adjournment.

COMMITTEES BY CATEGORY

A ssociation committees fall into four basic categories:

1. Governance. Although the average board totals 27 members, sizes can range from just 3 members to as many as 75. Depending on the size of the board and the frequency with which it meets, an executive committee or committee of officers may be empowered to act on behalf of the full board. The larger its board and the less frequent its meetings, the more likely an association is to have such a group, which averages 7 members.

   Other key governance committees are a nominating committee, a bylaws committee, and a finance or budget committee.

2. Policy. In organizations that maintain a significant advocacy role, policy committees tend to focus on the ongoing study of major issues confronting the association. They provide resolutions to the board or house of delegates related to the association's stance in the public policy arena.

   These committees may also address internal policies, such as investment guidelines, membership qualifications, and so forth.

3. Program. These committees are affiliated with association projects, programs, and activities that have some definable output, such as a scientific program, educational curriculum, publications, or research and statistics. Program committees may be as small as one person or as large as several hundred, depending on the tasks to be accomplished. For example, evaluating 2,000 abstracts within a few weeks and sorting them down to 450 would require a large scientific program committee.

4. Networking. This category refers to a group of individual professionals or corporate representatives who come together to communicate with one another, not necessarily to generate projects, programs, activities, or policies relevant to the rest of the organization. Networking committees can be quite large and are often formed to meet the needs of a subset of the membership.

A different type of agenda would maximize the association boards' and committees' effectiveness. For example, the most important activity undertaken by a board or other deliberative body is to take action on significant items; its second priority is to discuss matters that will require action at a subsequent meeting. The more significant the proposed action, the more time and meetings needed to build a consensus. The final obligation of the board is to stay up-to-date on association activities that don't require action.

Given those parameters, a meeting agenda ought to look like this:

I.   Call to order and establishment of a quorum.

II.   Approval of the agenda. (This may include a consent calendar—a list of items assembled by the presiding officer and the staff and perceived as non-controversial or mere housekeeping matters; the board adopts the items with a single vote. Individual members, however, have the right to remove from the calendar those items they wish to discuss more fully.)

III.   Action items. This is a list of actions or proposed resolutions that the board will be called on to decide at this meeting.

IV.   Discussion items that require debate or discussion in anticipation of a decision at a future date.

V.   Information items, preferably presented in writing rather than orally.

VI.   Adjournment.

Background and supporting material should match the agenda, meaning that each action item should have a separate cover sheet that describes:

- The source of the resolution.
- The language of the resolution.
- The steps taken to develop the resolution.
- A rationale for decision.
- A statement of the resources that would be required if the resolution were adopted.
- An opportunity for noting the disposition of the resolution.

SELECTION AND ELECTION

When it comes to electing board members and officers, you'll find as many variations as there are types of organizations. With charities, for instance, the board is usually charged with identifying and recruiting new members, with the active participation of the chief staff executive. In most professional societies, board members serve either as elected delegates of an interest group or geographic region or as at-large members. For trade associations, the elective process must maintain a balance between a few large dues payers and the many smaller organizations found within their membership.

Some organizations present a single slate for election (although most have some mechanism for placing nominees on the ballot by petition), while others nominate more than one candidate for an office. The argument for a single slate is that losers of a contested election may become disgruntled and withdraw from active participation. On the other hand, say critics, proposing a slate for election means that a small clique—typically the nominating committee—is able to seize power, resist change, and ignore diverse opinions. ■

Staff Structure and Roles

Key Points

- With technological advances, such as local area computer networks, have come more fluid communication among staff members, easier access to information, and a flattening of the organizational chart.

- A unique characteristic of association work for staff specialists is simultaneously reporting to a staff supervisor and working with volunteers who perceive themselves as able to direct staff activities.

- The chief staff executive shapes the association's culture and, during the hiring process, should remain sensitive to how a prospective employee would fit into it.

Managing employees presents challenges no matter what your work environment. The association sector, however, requires some special considerations that typically don't arise in for-profit organizations.

Most associations' activities fall into a common set of functional patterns: liaison with the organization's governing body; finance and administration; publications and communication; meetings, conventions, and trade shows; research and statistics; government relations; membership record keeping and membership marketing; and perhaps others. Staff structure and roles typically align with these functions.

In view of all the varied activities, it's important to note that the average association has fewer than 10 paid staff members. In smaller associations particularly, employees must exhibit a range of talents and an ability to juggle multiple priorities to be effective. Of course, versatility has its limits. At a minimum, staffing levels must provide for general clerical support, maintenance of membership records, filing of appropriate forms with state and federal governments, working with the board and crucial committees, and some regular communication with the membership.

The staff size and structure of an individual membership organization whose primary benefits are periodicals and educational meetings will look very different from those of a trade association with relatively few large corporate members who consider government relations the principal membership benefit. In the latter type of organization, the chief staff executive frequently plays an advocacy role, and the first support staff hired would manage clerical functions, communication, and meetings. In the former type of organization, where communication is key, the chief staff executive might come from a field such as public relations or journalism.

Responding to Growth

All successful associations, regardless of their mission or focus, experience similar growing pains. As the association's work expands, additional employees are added to handle the various functional areas. Controlled growth can be achieved either by hiring part-time personnel until workloads justify a full-time staff member or by outsourcing some functions.

Using outside suppliers to handle occasional, large tasks can significantly ease the pressures on a small staff. Some organizations, for example, use outside firms to produce publications or to handle much of the planning related to meetings. In recent years, many associations are making extensive use of outsourcing. According to *Policies & Procedures in Association Management* (1996), 68 percent of associations outsource some of their activities, especially payroll, computer training, magazine production, and surveys and research.

Many small and mid-sized associations contract for staff and other services with an association management company (AMC), which may have a variety of associations and organizations as clients. Each client has a designated chief staff executive, who coordinates governance activities and provides access to a centralized professional staff offering such services as meeting management, publications, finance, and administration. With the development of special interest groups within their memberships, large associations in particular have created the equivalent of an in-house multiple management firm.

For example, the American Trucking Associations, in Alexandria, Virginia, has several subordinate organizations related to intermodal transport (land/sea containers) and long-distance trucking, to name a few. Each group has its own organizational structure and a designated staff liaison who provides staff services. The American College of Radiology, in Reston, Virginia, manages a number of radiological sub-specialty societies.

In most associations with state or local chapters, the chapters incorporate separately and make their own decisions related to staffing. In fact, because of their smaller size, chapters often are directed by association management companies, while their parent organizations have full-time staffs.

Technological advances, such as networked computers, have begun to affect organizational structures and hierarchies. With more fluid communication among staff members—and easier access to information—has come a flattening of the organizational chart. Classic management theory assumes that the optimum ratio of subordinates to managers is 6:1. Armed with better information, second-tier managers can significantly increase their level of professionalism and their ability to supervise a greater number of people. As a result, even the largest associations need have no more than three or four levels of management.

Managing the Staff Specialist

Associations hire staff specialists for their demonstrated skills—the ability to plan and carry out meetings, write and edit publications, lobby governments and agencies, and so forth. Consequently, senior association managers often face the challenge of effectively overseeing employees who know much more than they do about an area.

KEEPING IT LEGAL

Like every other employer in the United States, an association is prohibited from discriminating against current or potential employees on the basis of race, color, sex, national origin, religion, and disability. During the hiring process, questions must remain focused on the skills and characteristics of the candidate that relate to his or her ability to accomplish the job. Anything else carries the potential for a discrimination lawsuit.

Staying up-to-date on laws that affect human resources requires constant monitoring. The association trade press and ASAE are two resources, and outside legal counsel often provides helpful updates on the issues.

Despite legal restrictions, some legitimate interview questions can reveal much about the person's motivation and capacity to do the work. They include:

■ This job requires frequent travel and overtime work. Do you foresee any difficulties doing this?

■ What were your responsibilities in your previous jobs? What did you like most/least about them?

■ Why did you leave your previous job?

■ Would you require any reasonable accommodation to do this job?

■ What kinds of people do you find most difficult to work with?

■ Tell me about a time when you were highly motivated at work. What was happening?

It's not unusual, for instance, for a chief staff executive with precious little technical background to supervise a computer specialist who maintains the local area network and decides which software packages the association will use. Executives in that position often elect to consult with a colleague who has more expertise in the subject area. They also ask a lot of questions and—as with any supplier, in-house or outside—insist on clear answers.

Another common problem is that staff specialists may exhibit more loyalty to their specialty area than to the broader field of association management. A 1993 study conducted by Bob Jones, *How to Keep and Motivate Staff Specialists*, found that 91 percent of new employees knew "practically nothing" or "relatively little" about the association field when they took their first job. This is hardly surprising, as virtually no one heads off to college with the goal of becoming an association executive. Instead, they study fields such as journalism or finance and continue to identify with those areas after being employed by an association. Indeed, Jones' research showed that "interest in my functional area" was just as important as "interest in the issues of the industry or profession" when an association job offer came along.

Staff specialists can certainly develop a broader perspective of association issues and operations, especially when senior managers share relevant information. This can be accomplished effectively through a thorough orientation program that introduces new employees to the organization's mission, philosophy, and history, as well as the association field as a whole.

The Jones study found that more than 70 percent of respondents received one day—or less—of orientation when they took their first association job. What's more, just over half (57 percent) of associations offer orientation to new staff members. Considering that 63 percent of staff specialists are hired with no background knowledge of association management, it's easy to see why many continue to see themselves as writers or accountants rather than association executives.

A unique characteristic of association work for staff specialists is simultaneously reporting to a staff supervisor and working with volunteers who perceive themselves as able to direct staff activities. Problems can arise when staff specialists find themselves caught between staff supervisors' and volunteers' disparate expectations and pressures to perform.

The association's senior governance can ease this dilemma by simply clarifying the respective roles of volunteers and staff and emphasizing that the ultimate responsibility for employee performance rests on the chief staff executive. In other words, employees are accountable through the staff structure; only the chief staff executive answers directly to the board. In turn, the chief staff executive should develop a mechanism to help staff members identify priorities for action and encourage an open discussion of roles and relationships between staff and volunteers.

Compensation and Motivation

How much should employees be paid? For guidance, association executives can turn to compensation surveys produced by allied societies—state or local societies of association executives—associations of human resources managers, and commercial sources. Because many jobs in larger associations are similar to positions in the for-profit sector, studies by the Executive Compensation Service and other local business surveys may prove helpful in evaluating an organization's compensation policies.

In addition, every two years, the American Society of Association Executives (ASAE) conducts an extensive survey on salaries and fringe benefits offered to association employees by position. The 2001 edition of *The Association Executive Compensation & Benefits Study* identified the average total compensation for these position titles as follows:

Chief Executive Officer	$105,500
Deputy Chief Executive	$ 90,000
Government/Lobbying Director	$ 82,000
Meetings and Expositions Director	$ 56,386
Membership Development Director	$ 55,000
Publishing Director	$ 60,119

Salary and benefits are both extrinsic motivators—although important, they're external considerations. Intrinsic motivators—those that come from within a person—also play an important role in keeping staff members satisfied. For example, someone may value a position because it offers interesting work, opportunities for promotion and growth, or the chance to work with creative and innovative people. To recruit and retain talented employees, especially when unemployment is low, some associations offer job-sharing arrangements, flextime, and telecommuting options. Each job candidate may have a different motivating factor.

Anyone who has had more than one employer can attest that organizations have different cultures, much like people have different personalities. It falls to the chief staff executive to shape the association's culture and, during the hiring process, be sensitive to how the prospective employee would fit into it. That's not to say an association should hire a set of clones, but rather that it should develop a mix of personality styles appropriate to its culture.

Since the late 1980s, a host of new terms related to individual motivation has entered the management lexicon. Matrix management, total quality management, management by objectives, process reengineering, self-guided teams, quality circles—no matter what the name, each approach emphasizes the fact that employees will seek responsibility and opportunities to achieve if a job effectively uses their skills and talents.

To motivate people, managers must assess their competency, train them appropriately, give them substantive responsibilities that stretch their competence, and recognize and reward them in ways appropriate to their performance. Managers also have the responsibility of reaching agreement with employees about the goals they desire to achieve and to "coach" from the sidelines.

Because of the complexity of many organizational objectives, association employees must work effectively and collegially both with other staff members and volunteers. In evaluating a prospective employee, the manager should consider the amount and intensity of the team effort the position requires. Some jobs in larger associations are compatible with people who like to close the door, turn off the phone, and focus intensely on a particular task. Most of the time, however, association work requires constant team effort and interpersonal communication. Therefore, other skills being equal, the person who can operate well in a position with discontinuity, ambiguity, and shared responsibility is better suited for the association environment. ■

Volunteer Management

Key Points

■ Baby Boomers and Gen-Xers exhibit qualitative as well as quantitative differences from the generations that preceded them. These differences have profound implications for the recruitment of volunteers.

■ Volunteers are needed to get the job done, foster commitment to the association, and develop future leaders.

■ The more realistic the expectations when a volunteer signs on, the greater the likelihood that the volunteer experience will be enjoyable and productive for all parties involved.

The most profound social trend of the late 20th and early 21st centuries is the archetypal "pig in the python"— the Baby Boom generation. While different authors have proposed various start and end dates for this population surge, Baby Boomers were, by and large, born between 1946 and 1964. Because of its sheer size—76 million Americans—this generation has dominated the public consciousness and significantly influenced American society.

It all started with a tremendous growth of diaper services in the late 1940s, followed by a boom in construction for grammar, junior high, and high schools. Then came rapid changes on campuses as rebellious Boomers went to college in the '60s and '70s. In the following decade, Boomer couples flexed their earnings muscles and began having families of their own, giving rise to a "boomlet" and a focus on childcare alternatives.

Beyond their sheer size, however, Boomers exhibit qualitative as well as quantitative differences from the generations that preceded them. Sociologists and researchers have noted that Boomers, for example, boast a higher percentage of two-income families and tend to marry and have children later in life. They also have a higher incidence of divorce and single-parent families, both of which can add to responsibilities at home. They form the most highly educated generation in the history of the United States and are accustomed to a great deal of attention.

These characteristics—two incomes, high divorce, later marriage and children—are also characteristic of the Gen-Xers, born between 1965 and 1985. The younger Xers are comfortable with technology, having grown up with personal computers as a common tool. Many have found community on the Internet.

Recruitment Challenges

These characteristics all have profound implications for the recruitment of volunteers. Traditional volunteers, particularly at the national level, have been in their mid-40s to mid-50s. That used to be the age when the children had left home and their parents could focus on volunteer activities as a way of paying something back to their trade or profession.

But at midlife, many Boomers have young children still at home and, consequently, much less time for the collegiality of the volunteer experience. They prefer to get home in time to coach a child's soccer game or attend a PTA event rather
than attend a board meeting for another day.

And the younger Gen-Xers are just beginning their families.

Simultaneously, because the American healthcare system has lowered the
death rate from acute disease, Boomers now find themselves in a generational
sandwich—they're not only nurturing children but also supporting aging parents.
The Xers will face the same situation as they age.

Another stress on the volunteer system concerns the changing nature of organizations. Traditionally, the volunteers most involved in association activities were
professionals or mid- to upper-level managers. But beginning in the 1980s,
technological and economic changes led to a de-layering or downsizing of
middle management in many American companies. Concerns about holding on
to a job—or finding another one in a rapidly changing and competitive
marketplace—clearly take precedence over volunteer activities. As more companies go global and are owned by non-U.S. corporations with a different appreciation of the role of associations, support for participation may ebb.

The fitness craze offers yet another competitor for the time of Boomers and
Gen-Xers. People who spend several hours a week exercising their bodies have less
time available for volunteer service. So just as the three key issues for retailers are
location, location, and location, the problem for the volunteer recruiter targeting
the younger generations is time, time, and time.

Importance of Volunteers

Given the difficulty in getting people to volunteer, every organization must ask,
"Why do we want volunteers in the first place?" Three answers come to mind:

1. To get the job done. This answer immediately prompts two further questions:
"What job, exactly?" and "Does it really need to be done at all?" Difficulties in
recruiting volunteers may be a blessing in disguise, motivating the organization to
seriously look at the activities it undertakes. A project, program, or activity traditionally done by volunteers could be done some other way, perhaps by staff. Or it's
possible that volunteers would be more inclined to commit additional money to
an activity rather than additional time. Another option might be to change the job
asked of volunteers, either by making it smaller, shorter in duration, or more
meaningful.

After taking a serious look at their volunteer structures, many associations have
decided to eliminate many of their standing committees and instead organize ad
hoc task forces. They've found it much easier to recruit volunteers by saying, in
effect, "We have this specific, meaningful, and important task for you to undertake. Here is how your work will contribute to the achievement of our goals and

accomplish our mission. The required time commitment is limited, and when you're done, we will disband the group with the recognition and thanks of the entire organization."

This approach certainly differs from the ordinary volunteer assignment, which seems to be, "Come serve on the Widget Committee, which meets four times a year. It's a four-year term, and we aren't really sure that anything important will come up. But if it does, we'll be ready."

A NEW MODEL

The American Animal Hospital Association (AAHA), Denver, Colorado, had a complex infrastructure that included many standing committees and numerous positions for volunteers to serve as liaisons between the national organization and its grassroots membership. Realizing the system was not working, AAHA decided to realign volunteer responsibilities.

After eliminating the liaisons and many of the existing standing committees, the association created the Committee of 100. The committee—which, in fact, is not limited to 100 people—is used for three purposes:

■ Members of the committee agree to respond to quarterly surveys on matters of significance to the association. This enables AAHA to tap into the opinions of key members around the country.

■ Members, who are surveyed for their skills and interests, serve as a national talent pool for ad hoc committees. Since AAHA eliminated most of its standing committees, ad hoc committees have proliferated, although they do not come close to the total number of committees that existed in the past. Recruiting members for the ad hoc groups is easier than before because the time commitment is limited and the groups convene only when they have something significant to do.

■ In limited numbers, members are invited to participate in leadership development activities sponsored by the national organization.

AAHA drops from the committee those members who fail to respond to the surveys, repeatedly decline to serve on ad hoc committees, or refuse invitations to leadership training. This design meets the needs of both the association and the individuals who are truly interested in volunteering.

2. To foster commitment. Volunteers strengthen the level of their commitment to the organization—the more they do for the association, the more loyalty they feel.

Some organizations have succeeded in fostering commitment through means other than volunteerism. For example, the National Federation of Independent Business (NFIB), in Nashville, Tennessee, regularly mails questionnaires so members can provide input on public policy matters pending before Congress. Members of Congress respond to the individual NFIB members whose names they have been given, thus closing the loop and validating the individual member's continued participation in the program.

Offering a "golden handcuff"—a product or service unattainable elsewhere—builds loyalty as well. The Ontario Chiropractic Association, Mississauga, is the sole source of chiropractic professional liability insurance in the Canadian province and, under Canadian law, may offer it only to members. Other organizations offer research results or statistical information that members find invaluable.

3. To develop future leaders. The real question is, "Do we really develop leaders, or do we give them the opportunity to develop themselves?" Relatively few organizations structure their leadership development activities in a rational manner; the majority allows volunteers to self-select for leadership opportunities and do little formal development. Avoiding this "catch as catch can" approach should be a primary responsibility of current leaders and staff as they look ahead to developing people who can successfully lead the association in the future.

Motivational Theories

To recruit and retain active volunteers, it helps to understand what motivates people in general. Abraham Maslow developed the theory that people have a "hierarchy of needs" that arises in a certain order; their higher level needs don't become apparent until lower level needs have been met. Maslow's hierarchy, from base (lower-level needs) to tip (higher-level needs), goes like this: survival, safety, affiliation, self-esteem and the esteem of others, and self-actualization.

According to Maslow, it's difficult, if not impossible, to motivate people by offering them opportunities for affiliation and collegiality if their basic survival is at stake. You cannot expect people to be concerned about the esteem of others if they're starving or homeless. Likewise, people who feel insecure because of intense job pressure are less likely to volunteer just to meet a higher need for affiliation or self-esteem.

Another motivational theorist, Frederick Herzberg, assessed what motivates people by simply asking them, "When you were motivated on the job, what was going on? And when you were dissatisfied with your work, what was happening?" He found that certain conditions or behaviors, when present in the workplace, made people dissatisfied. Those included poor policy and administration, inadequate technical or interpersonal supervision, poor working conditions, a perceived lack of fairness in salary, poor relationships with one's peers, difficulties in one's personal life, difficult relationships with one's subordinates, inadequate status, and anxiety over security.

Interestingly, when the dissatisfaction factors were ameliorated, employees did not become highly motivated; they simply were not dissatisfied. What motivated people was a sense of achievement, recognition linked to one's achievement, tasks suited to the individual's skill and inclinations, a sense that one was responsible and in control of one's actions, an opportunity for professional advancement, and personal growth. These same motivators are equally powerful within the context of the volunteer experience.

REASONS FOR INVOLVEMENT

Why do you volunteer? Ask people that question, and these answers usually follow:

1. I want to pay back the field that has been good to me.

2. It's an opportunity for me to increase my knowledge. My interaction with other more knowledgeable individuals will improve my ability to function in my trade or profession.

3. I'm doing it for the contacts. In the long term, the relationships that I build through my volunteer involvement will help develop my career.

4. Volunteer experience gives me an opportunity to express my values, to involve myself in an activity that I think is meaningful and important.

A fifth possibility typically remains unspoken: I get involved in volunteer activities as a means of therapy, a way of playing out difficulties in my personal life.

Clarifying the Commitment

In view of Herzberg's findings, and assuming that members have reached at least the need for affiliation on Maslow's hierarchy, let's look at what volunteers want to know before making a commitment to their association.

- What does the job entail? This goes beyond a simple job description to include a clear understanding of how much time is required and who will cover the costs of participation. Many people have agreed to serve on a volunteer committee or board only to discover that, in addition to the time spent preparing for and attending meetings, they're expected to participate in special events and contribute to fund-raising campaigns simply because they're leaders.

    When the reality of a volunteer role proves alarmingly different from the expectations, members are less likely to jump at the next volunteer opportunity that comes along. As a result, honesty is the best policy.

- Will the work help or hinder me in my career? Volunteers may be intrigued by the possibility of making new contacts or concerned that the position will raise a supervisor's hackles by requiring significant time away from their job. It's best to address such concerns by pointing to the experience of other volunteers and emphasizing that leadership skills developed through volunteerism can be used on the job.

- How will I fit in with the others? Few volunteers like the thought of sitting quietly for six months until they can figure out who the other board or committee members are. Associations can help allay these fears by providing social opportunities for volunteers to meet and learn about one's colleagues before getting down to their work.

- Is the job meaningful? The volunteer, not the organization, defines what's meaningful. But the organization needs to understand potential volunteers well enough to place them in positions that will most likely meet their needs and capacities. This can be done, in part, by being very clear about the task to be accomplished and allowing people to make their own choices.

- What kind of recognition can I expect? Traditionally, recognition within associations has been based on title or position rather than performance—all committee members get the same certificate and all committee chairs get the same small plaque, regardless of whether they showed up for meetings or did any work between meetings.

   With volunteer expectations changing, associations must rethink how volunteers are recognized and strive to make it relevant to achievement. That may mean evaluating volunteers and recognizing only those who really do the work. Those who prove unproductive would either be encouraged to hold jobs that fit their skills better or not be recruited again.

- Will I get training? Because they may worry about "playing catch up" when joining a committee that's already been working on a problem or have no experience in chairing a committee, potential volunteers should be informed about the extent of training and orientation they will receive. Orientation should cover both the specific association and the nature of associations in general. Additional training aimed at helping the volunteer be productive might include the history, policies, and procedures of the association as well as details on the volunteer's particular role.

- Will I grow from the experience? Associations must be prepared to tell volunteers how their involvement can lead to significant personal growth either in knowledge or experience. Otherwise, recruitment will be difficult.

- What help will I get from staff? The relationship between staff and volunteers, a source of tension in many associations, is rarely discussed explicitly. Based on experience in other organizations, volunteers may expect staff to handle all meeting arrangements, development of the agenda, and minutes. They need to know—before accepting a position—whether staff has the same understanding. If a volunteer agrees to chair a committee and then discovers that there's no staff support, he or she either won't do the job, will be unhappy doing it (and therefore probably won't volunteer again), or will just make life difficult for staff.

- How efficiently will we operate? Some associations have traditionally viewed volunteer service as more of an opportunity for social interaction than decision making. Because of their other responsibilities and the nature of the society in which they operate, however, Boomers and Gen-Xers tend to see the volunteer experience as a way of accomplishing meaningful things.

The way an association structures its meetings and the venues it selects communicate a commitment to either efficiency or collegiality. For example, some associations have shifted away from resorts in favor of using airport hotels for business meetings.

Newer volunteers expect a greater use of technology to support their volunteer participation. They will expect the association to make use of teleconferencing, Web-based decision making, listservers, and other tools to help the group do its work.

■ What else is in it for me? Baby Boomers and Gen-Xers in particular keep this question in the back of their minds even if they rarely ask it. A good answer—whether it's increased visibility in the profession or the opportunity to hone personal skills—will help you attract good volunteers.

These questions have no standard answers. Each organization must formulate its own responses and communicate them clearly as part of the recruitment effort. The more realistic the expectations when a volunteer signs on, the greater the likelihood that the volunteer experience will be enjoyable and productive for all parties involved.

If addressed honestly, some of these questions may have discouraging answers. You may discover, for example, that all volunteer positions within your association are lengthy, time consuming, burdensome, and lacking in recognition. And if you can't attract volunteers to the jobs you have, it's time to change the jobs.

It can help to think about volunteer recruitment and management from a marketing standpoint by asking, "What are your needs, and how can we organize to deliver them?" Or, put another way to potential volunteers, "If you could design a volunteer effort that would be interesting and rewarding to you, what would it look like?" ■

Budgeting and Finance

Key Points

- According to a study of critical competencies, the number one skill needed in association work is control over finances.

- In its simplest form, the budget projects the amount and sources of income (revenues), plus the amount of estimated expenditures and where that money will be allocated (expenses).

- Management reports—including the balance sheet, income and expense statement, and cash flow statement—keep stakeholders abreast of financial developments.

Many people select a career in association management because they believe it will enable them to put their communication and "people" skills to good use. Because they're entering the nonprofit arena, they may think they can avoid dealing with numbers. The latter assumption doesn't prove true.

In fact, the number one skill needed in association work is managing finances. That finding emerged from *Critical Competencies of Association Executives* (1988), a study commissioned by the American Society of Association Executives (ASAE). The study, conducted by Lawrence Leiter & Company, showed that both association executives and volunteers agreed on the importance of financial skills. Yet, while a chief staff executive who can't control the organization's finances is more likely to incur the wrath of the board—and ultimately to lose his or her job—people skills are also important. In other words, financial skills are the mark of a good manager—but on their own aren't sufficient and must be supplemented by other skills.

Financial control builds on one basic concept: Finances must be properly accounted for. First, legal requirements, such as tax returns, cannot be met without having good accounting practices in place. Second, the "owners" of the association—the members—rightfully demand to know the financial circumstances of their property. In addition, efficient and effective management of the entire organization proves impossible without an understanding of the overall financial situation.

The accounting system must be structured to meet all these needs simultaneously. That, of course, means paperwork.

The Budget

The budget is the financial expression of an association's plans for a defined upcoming period, usually one year. In its simplest form, the budget projects the amount and sources of income (revenues), plus the amount of estimated expenditures and where that money will be allocated (expenses). Having data on the current year's budget and actual numbers to date, as well as full information about prior years, makes budget preparation considerably easier; many types of association activities and expenditures remain much the same from year to year.

The revenue side of the budget can look strikingly similar from one association to another. It typically includes these revenue streams: membership dues, advertising income, sale of publications, fees for conferences and educational programs, exhibit space rentals, royalties, and interest income. As an organization grows, these categories may be broken down further. For instance, dues from various categories of membership may be projected separately, and registration fees for smaller meetings may be separated from those for the annual convention.

Many small organizations use a functional budget, in which the expense side of the budget is itemized according to the goods or services received.

As organizations grow, they should adopt a program budget that allocates expenses not just by functional area but also by the program or particular product for which the money was spent. For example, printing and postage costs would be broken out into membership recruitment and retention, educational programs, the annual meeting, individual conferences or publications, and so forth.

Until 1994, organizations could keep their books without allocating costs if they had no unrelated business income—that is, no income derived from a trade or business that is regularly carried on but not substantially related to their tax-exempt purpose. Those with unrelated business income to report had to distinguish only between taxable and nontaxable items. But when the U.S. Congress passed a law saying that dues used for lobbying were no longer deductible, all associations engaged in lobbying activities had to begin earmarking expenses closely.

Without allocating costs fully, it's impossible to know whether individual projects, programs, or activities are returning net revenue to the organization or draining its resources. Organizations with a functional budget know only the direct costs—money paid to outside suppliers—never the true costs of individual activities. Staff costs are the largest association expense, representing about one-third (33.7 percent) of total association revenue. The value of staff time should be allocated to the programs on which they work. Copying, phone, and postage costs can be easily allocated through the use of metering and coding devices. Understanding the true costs makes it easier to decide which activities to expand, revise, or drop.

Consequently, every organization with more than one project, program, or activity should develop a program-oriented budget with reasonable provisions for cost allocation. In the days of pencil-and-paper bookkeeping this might have been unrealistic. But accounting software now makes it easy to adopt the more useful budget form.

In addition to laying out the dollars and cents, both functional and program budgets may describe the assumptions on which the numbers are based. For

ITEMIZED EXPENSES

These categories of expenses typically appear in a functional budget:

Personnel Salaries—Exempt Staff

Personnel Salaries—Non-Exempt Staff

Personnel Salaries—Temporary Staff Commissions

Personnel Benefits

Personnel Taxes and Workers' Compensation

Personnel Training and Development

Dues, Subscriptions, and Publications

Accounting Fees

Professional and Consulting Fees—Computer/Technology

Professional and Consulting Fees—Legal

Professional and Consulting Fees—Other

Occupancy—Rent

Telephone

Office Equipment and Supplies

Postage and Shipping

Printing and Photocopying Costs

Travel—Staff

Travel—Non-Staff

Meetings—Meals Provided at Events

Meetings—Entertainment

Meetings—Equipment Rental

Meetings—Facilities Rental

Meetings—Speaking Fees

Meetings—Other

Insurance (excludes employee benefits)

Technology—Annual Hardware Expenditure

Technology—Annual Software Expenditure

Technology—Web Site Design/Maintenance

Technology—Outside Service Bureau

Depreciation and Amortization

Cost of Goods Sold

Taxes—Federal Income Taxes

Taxes—State and Local Taxes

Other Expense

Source: ASAE Operating Ratio Report, *Eleventh Edition.*

example, supporting information for a budget line item related to an educational program might project the number of attendees and the various registration fees they would pay (such as discounted "early bird" registration versus on-site). The expense section would then describe the printing, postage, and mailing costs related to promoting the meeting; the value of salaries and fringe benefits for staff involved in producing the meeting; room rental; food and beverage charges; audiovisual charges; speakers' honoraria; and so forth. Requiring this detail forces staff to think through their assumptions and produces a more realistic budget.

Many budgets also contain background or historical numbers, including the previous year's actuals, current year's budget, and projected final numbers. For instance, if budget assumptions are fully integrated with the dollar figures, the columns across the budget sheets might read:

1. Budget Revenue

2. Budget Expense

3. Assumptions

4. Current Budget Revenue (and Expense)

5. Adjusted Current Budget Revenue (and Expense)

6. Last Year's Actual Revenue (and Expense)

When budget figures differ significantly from historical data—or when no historical data exist to support a new activity—more detailed explanations are necessary. Those additional comments might appear on the page across from the corresponding budget numbers or be grouped together and keyed to pages in the budget document.

Staff and Volunteer Participation

The roles staff and volunteers play in the budgeting process can vary widely. Some organizations make staff completely responsible for budget preparation, leaving the board of directors to merely review the finished product. In other associations, volunteers become intimately involved in developing the budget for their respective committees or programs.

A budget and finance committee is especially important for involving volunteers in the budgeting process. Many crucial decisions related to allocating resources and establishing organizational priorities are made at this level. Often, the incoming chief elected officer serves on the committee to become more familiar with the association's financial structure.

The budget process can be extremely time consuming and frustrating, starting nearly a year in advance and forcing hard choices because the demand for resources tends to outstrip the supply. One danger is that the budget and finance committee will make reckless and unwise decisions in an attempt to satisfy all the various demands. Committees have been known to arbitrarily raise revenue estimates to unrealistic levels to create a balanced budget.

When the committee's projections prove overly optimistic, however, staff members are usually held accountable. This can lead to low morale and high turnover among staff members who feel powerless. To avoid this problem, the budget and finance committee should establish policies for its operations, including a written budget philosophy that binds committee members and staff to exercise caution when estimating revenues and to be generous in estimating expenses. This approach can create both end-of-year surpluses and happier staff and members.

The Chart of Accounts

At the heart of an accounting system is the chart of accounts—a numbered list of programs or areas to which revenues and expenses will be allocated. Essentially, the chart of accounts groups money together under headings, such as Assets (current and fixed), Liabilities and Net Assets, and Revenues and Expenses. The chart should group information in a way that makes it easy to respond to the Internal Revenue Service's requests for information and to provide financial data to both members and management.

The association executive has the responsibility of describing to the accountant or financial consultant what the organization's needs are and then leaving that person to structure the system accordingly. For instance, the chart of accounts may be divided by department. This gives the department head the opportunity to be responsible for preparing the budget for the activities under his or her control and to be held accountable for results.

The chart of accounts should remain relatively stable; both auditors and members appreciate consistency. But the creation of a new project, program, or activity probably will generate a new account. As a result, when setting up a chart of accounts, most accountants leave unassigned numbers in several ranges to accommodate future growth and change.

Management Reports

Once the budgeting process is complete, management is obliged to regularly report to both members and leaders on how the money is coming in and where it's being spent. This information usually is presented to the membership annually, after the association's financial statements have been audited. The board typically receives a report at its meetings (at least quarterly), while the budget and finance committee is informed at least quarterly and sometimes monthly. Finally, staff members find it helpful to have monthly reports for their ongoing work.

What information should the reports include? Remember that management reports are intended to keep stakeholders abreast of financial developments.

Because many budgets project income and expenses on a monthly basis, monthly reports offer a good chance to test the validity of the budget's predictions. Therefore, as actual figures become available, the management reports should provide the following data for both revenues and expenses:

- Current Month Actual
- Current Month Budget
- Year-to-Date Actual
- Year-to-Date Budget
- Year-to-Date Variance
- Annual Budget
- Year-to-Date Budget as a Percent of Total Budget
- Year-to-Date Actual as a Percent of Total Budget

  Management reports may include the following:

- Balance Sheet. Like a camera, the balance sheet freezes for a moment the constant changes in assets, liabilities, and net assets to provide a snapshot of the organization's financial condition. It describes what the association owns (total assets) as well as what it owes (total liabilities). Total assets always equal total liabilities plus the net assets.

  Net assets refers to the amount that would remain after the organization converted all its assets—including real property—into cash and paid off its debts. As a rule, the larger the net assets, the better the organization's financial position.

  By comparing the net assets to annual expenses (found in the income and expense statement), you'll see how long the organization could operate if it had no revenues coming in. Most organizations seek to have net assets of at least 50 percent of one year's expenditures. Also, by comparing the net assets to the "cash and equivalents" line on the asset side of the balance sheet, you'll have some idea of how liquid the organization is; that is, how many of its assets could be readily converted into cash should an emergency arise. A strong cash position and substantial net assets indicate that, at least on the day the snapshot was taken, the organization was in sound financial shape.

  Another way to analyze a balance sheet is to compare it to those of similar organizations. Organizational operating ratios—the average revenues and expenses as a percentage of total income—offer financial and operational benchmarks that come in handy when planning and evaluating an association's operations.

- Income and Expense Statement. It's not enough to know how much cash an organization has or the level of its net assets. Members also want to know where that money came from and where it's being spent. The income and expense statement is usually organized by program area, such as publications, meetings and conventions, and so forth, so it's easy to see how much income a particular activity generated and how much it cost to produce.

- Cash Flow Statement. Also referred to as the Statement of Changes in Financial Position, this document provides the information bridge between the Income and Expense Statement and the Balance Sheet. It reflects the sources of funds and how their expenditure affected accounts on the Balance Sheet.
- Audited Statement. This is actually a collection of three other documents—the balance sheet, income and expense statement, and cash flow statement—that gains added credibility because it is prepared once a year by an outside certified public accountant.

Truly understanding an organization's financial condition requires reading the footnotes in the annual audited statement. They usually detail information that pertains to financial practices.

Investment Policies

Associations need to establish policies for the investment of their money, particularly the accumulated net assets or reserves. ASAE's *Operating Ratio Report* (11th edition) indicates that about half of the organizations surveyed have reserve/equity policies in place. Such statements vary in their content, but most set some limits on the kinds of investments that are permitted. Associations often have different policies governing the investment of operating cash, long-term reserves, and short-term reserves. ■

Marketing Basics

- Marketing, which is based on the idea of finding a need and filling it, focuses not on the product but on the market itself.

- Attempts to assess market needs help avoid offering products and programs for which no market exists and can also reveal unexpected needs.

- Research often revolves around the Four Ps of marketing: product, price, promotion, and place.

Many associations hire staff specialists not just in specific areas, such as publications and meeting planning, but in the broader arena of marketing. Even associations that can't afford a specialist see the potential of applying business marketing principles to many functional areas, whether it's promoting a new book, drumming up interest in a meeting, or repositioning the value of membership itself.

Marketing discussions all too often focus on promotion—how the association can present its goods and services to potential customers in a way that leads them to make a purchase. But marketing goes far beyond mere promotion, and it shouldn't be confused with selling.

What's the distinction? In selling, the general approach of the business (or association) is to understand its own capabilities, create new products based on those capabilities, and then sell those products to whoever happens to be around. Ability and capacity drive production.

Marketing, which is based on the idea of finding a need and filling it, takes a fundamentally different approach. The focus is not on the product but on the market itself. A marketer will argue that, before creating a product or service, organizations must understand the nature and needs of their customers. Management's task then becomes marshaling an organization's resources to best fulfill those needs through the production of goods and services.

Defining the Market

In the larger business world, for-profit organizations can pursue any market they choose. In trade associations and professional societies, however, the impulse is to define the market as the membership—the businesses or individuals qualified to join under the bylaws or articles of incorporation. Of course, these documents can be changed or the definition of membership could be recast as conditions warrant. But, deciding "who we want our members to be" is a crucial and strategic act.

Beyond their members, most associations have another major market: the individuals and organizations serving as suppliers to the membership. Although the ASAE *Operating Ratio Report* notes that the average association receives about 13 percent of its revenues from the supplier community (including exhibit fees for trade show displays, sponsorships, advertising in periodicals, and membership dues), some associations have a much higher proportion of income from the supplier market.

Another market to consider might be purchasers of the goods and services produced by members of the association. Cooperative associations, such as the Pork Producers Council, of Des Moines, Iowa, exist in large part to encourage the purchase of what their members produce. Even various government entities—legislative, administrative, and judicial—and the public at large represent markets whose needs must be understood by the organization.

Market Segmentation

Within the membership itself, associations often can identify subgroups or market segments with special needs. For example, the National Electrical Manufacturers Association, of Washington, D.C., identifies three distinct interest groups within its membership: makers of consumer, medical, and industrial goods. Subgroups also may form around demographic characteristics, such as groups for younger physicians, female attorneys, or students within the larger medical and legal associations.

Other associations segment their membership by the primary and secondary reasons members give for joining. Some just want the mailings, some want to be involved in governance, some want networking activities, some like to attend conferences. By identifying the various motives and needs of its members, the association can focus its efforts. For example, members who express little interest in attending meetings and conferences will not be sent expensive promotional material. Instead, they might be informed of the meeting and asked to send a reply postcard if they want further information.

Today's technology permits the capture of lots of information on the interests and purchasing habits of the membership. Mining that data can permit the organization to focus on meeting the needs of the individual member.

Market Research

Traditionally, associations assessed the needs of their members through a simple and informal survey of their leaders—the people active in governance or key committees. As long as an association remains small and its membership homogeneous, this technique works well. But as associations grow and their memberships become more diverse, the proportion of members who participate in leadership decreases. Those in leadership positions tend to be more committed to the association and frequently have different needs and expectations from those of the rank-and-file membership.

Taking a lesson from business, many associations now identify the needs of members and prospects through a variety of market research techniques. For instance, 44 percent of associations conduct member satisfaction surveys and 38 percent conduct needs assessments. They often begin their research by analyzing secondary sources of information, such as surveys and statistics compiled by outside firms, databases, library materials, the trade press, and government reports.

Primary research—gathering new data direct from the source—is often more specific and current than anything available in print. It doesn't have to be in the form of an elaborate (and expensive) scientific study; one of the best sources of primary research is an association's reception desk.

The more scientific market research falls into four basic categories:

1. Printed questionnaires. Pencil-and-paper questionnaires can be sent through the mail, by fax, or by e-mail or distributed to members attending an event. This technique's primary advantage is its ability to reach a large number of people at relatively low cost. Because of the typically large number of respondents, a properly conducted print survey rates high on the important issue of validity—with what certainty its results can be projected onto the larger population of members.

RESEARCH ON THE CHEAP

Information flow is a two-way street at the American Society of Association Executives, of Washington, D.C. Answering 16,000 requests for information a year may sound like a full-time job, but it's only half the picture for the staff of Information Central. By logging and categorizing each call, the department also gains insight into members' needs and concerns.

For each call that comes in, a staff member enters up to three keywords in Information Central's database. By regularly generating statistics on these keyword fields, the staff can spot trends in certain areas—for instance, the majority of calls in one month may focus on human resources or government relations issues. They pass these statistics to the program staff of ASAE's special interest sections, as well as to the convention, education, publishing, and membership departments, so that articles, books, and seminars can be planned to address areas of stated need.

Such research, which relies on "samples of convenience," lacks scientific validity; the phone calls aren't random and therefore don't represent an accurate statistical snapshot of what's on the minds of the entire association community. Still, the findings are enough to tell management where to concentrate its efforts to meet members' needs.

One weakness of this method involves methodology. Printed surveys are typically sent to a random selection of members. Randomization says that as long as every member of the population has an equal chance of being selected, the resulting sample will adequately reflect the many variations of that population in terms of demographics, values, attitudes, and so forth.

In other words, if 10 percent of an association's total membership is unhappy with its educational offerings, a truly random sample will include 10 percent who feel the same way. For instance, you couldn't guarantee a random sample by handing out survey forms to every 12th person who comes through the doors at an educational function—those already disillusioned with the education program won't be in attendance and therefore wouldn't have an equal chance of being sampled. Likewise, e-mail or Web site surveys may generate responses only from those who have access to or feel comfortable using the Internet.

The second major methodological concern is anonymity. Respondents who believe they can be identified, perhaps through an e-mail address or fax number, are likely to give socially acceptable answers instead of sharing their true feelings.

The survey's design can also skew results. The wording of some questions, for example, might lead respondents to a desired answer ("Are you in favor of attempts to tamper with the constitutional right to bear arms?") or force them into an either/or choice ("What is the better way to improve American education: increase teacher salaries or lengthen the school year?"). Other mistakes that destroy the validity of data include forcing a single answer to a two-part question ("How do you feel about our newsletter and magazine?") and offering an answer scale that is unbalanced or incomplete ("How would you rate this convention on the following scale: outstanding, good, or adequate?").

Selecting a valid sample and designing a good questionnaire require some expertise. Consultants can help design surveys that have statistical validity. Software packages also can help in the design process, in addition to performing both simple and sophisticated analyses of the resulting data.

2. Telephone interviews bring in results quicker than mail surveys but can be twice as costly because of the need to call many people to reach a valid response rate. Another consideration is whether members welcome or have an aversion to telephone contact at home or on the job.

3. Face-to-face interviews have a big advantage over printed surveys—people find it harder to refuse a human being than to throw away a piece of paper that asks the same questions. That personal contact can boost the response rate. In addition, face-to-face interviews can provide both hard statistical data as well as more in-depth, open-ended information.

On the other hand, such interviews are expensive because of the time-consuming, one-on-one interaction involved. Also, courtesy bias can creep into the interview—the interviewee gives the "right" or acceptable answer because he or she wants to be liked by the interviewer.

4. Focus groups, also referred to as group interviews, use a trained facilitator to lead a small group (eight to ten people) through a discussion of significant issues. Unlike the other three techniques, this one yields qualitative results that cannot be widely generalized because the survey sample is so small. On the other hand, focus groups permit you to ask probing questions and gain a deeper understanding of issues.

Some organizations use focus groups to pinpoint areas of interest or concern that they can investigate further with quantitative research techniques. Many associations use their annual meeting as an opportunity to convene a number of focus groups from various market segments, but it can be difficult to assemble a group of people as opposed to scheduling individual interviews. Moreover, participants in a focus group held at an annual meeting are not representative of the association as a whole. You will only be interviewing members who are committed enough to come to the meeting.

Even though business has conducted in-depth market research for many years, catastrophic misreadings of the marketplace still occur—just think of the Edsel or New Coke. In fact, the number of product launches each year is much higher than the success rate, even among those handled by experienced firms with huge research budgets. Research, in other words, doesn't guarantee success.

In addition, not all proposed products or services warrant significant market research efforts. If the incremental cost to launch the product is low and the downside risk minimal, market research may cost more than the resulting data are worth.

Despite these caveats, routine attempts to assess market needs will not only help avoid offering products and programs for which no market exists but also reveal unexpected needs. Those needs can then be met through the imaginative development of new or nontraditional products and services.

The Four Ps

Much of market research revolves around the Four Ps of marketing: product, price, promotion, and place.

PRODUCT

Associations typically pay close attention to the projects, programs, and activities offered to members. These generally fall into the following categories: publications, education and meetings, voluntary standards, and research and statistics.

At first glance, these items may appear to be an organization's primary products. But closer examination often reveals that the real product offered by most associations is information. Publications and meetings are merely different ways of conveying information. As information providers, some associations face competition from the Internet. Many associations, however, feel less threatened because their information has achieved, over time, the aura of a brand name— a reputation for accuracy and reliability that provides a strong position in the marketplace. Too, technological advances are leading associations to deliver information differently, not necessarily via an event at a physical location or printed piece that has long been considered a core product (see Chapters 8, 9, and 17).

PRICE

Associations frequently use committees of members to help set prices for various products and services. Unfortunately, the first instinct of members is to see themselves as customers rather than business managers. As a result, they may try to keep prices as low as possible, regardless of the product's inherent value, often suggesting that all products be priced to break even or to return a modest profit.

Compounding this problem may be a financial process that doesn't fully allocate costs to projects, programs, or activities (see Chapter 5). In this case, an organization is not just foregoing profits it deserves but actually losing money on its core offerings to members. One solution involves rethinking and reformulating the organization's financial structure to identify the true cost of programs. Then a plan can be developed to achieve a modest profit above actual costs.

Another approach, value-based pricing, turns the pricing procedure on its head by looking at value to the customer rather than cost to the producer. The logic beyond this approach says that even a large profit is acceptable, provided the members who purchase the product or service feel they are receiving value in exchange for their money. A healthy return on these high-value activities provides funding for other programs that don't generate sufficient revenues on their own yet are important to the association's mission.

PROMOTION

Associations tend to rely on direct mail as the mainstay of their promotional activities. Although popular, direct mail may not be the most efficient or effective means of promotion. For example, telephone marketing can be useful, particularly for high-ticket items or events.

The National Federation of Independent Business (NFIB) has recognized that its target market—primarily small, local retailers—doesn't respond to direct mail or telemarketing. Instead, NFIB uses commissioned salespeople who make direct contact calls to sell first-time memberships as well as renewals. Other organizations have found that broadcast fax announcements or e-mail messages get members' attention—but members must have the appropriate equipment and be amenable to receiving information electronically.

PLACE

Also known as distribution, this aspect of marketing has begun to change for associations long accustomed to delivering products through the mail or by holding events for people to attend: The age of telecommunications demands a different delivery system for both information and education products. Some sophisticated associations are asking members how and where they wish to receive information and then customize the interaction accordingly. A few associations have chosen to only deliver information electronically, whether it's a membership promotion, an educational offering, or a publication. The move toward broadband will only accelerate that trend.

Formulating a Plan

Researching each of the Four Ps is not an end to itself. The results of market research, particularly in the area of new product development, ought to be combined with other research activities to develop a business plan.

A business plan typically covers two to five years and includes the following:

- Description of the product or service.
- Market analysis, including evaluations of the current market, the potential market, and the competition.
- Pricing, promotion, and distribution strategies.
- Budget, including projected sales and expenses and estimated cash flow. ■

Membership

- While individual membership organizations are likely to have a flat- or fixed-rate dues structure, trade associations typically assess dues based on some measure of size, volume, or wealth.

- Associations typically provide three types of benefits to members: advocacy; goods and services, including publications; and opportunities for volunteer involvement.

- To discover what prospects and members want out of membership, associations must ask them.

A conscious dedication to meet the needs of their members, whether individual or corporate, distinguishes trade associations and professional societies from other kinds of organizations. Although often established to serve a specific market, for-profit businesses generally allow themselves free rein to follow wherever the market leads. Charities, meanwhile, tend to primarily serve "clients" or "patients," who aren't usually integrated into their governance structures.

At the inception of any membership organization, two questions immediately spring up:

- What shall we charge people to belong?
- What will members receive in exchange for their dues?

As the organization grows and changes, both questions bear reconsidering from time to time.

Setting Dues

Dues revenue represents the largest single source of association income. According to the ASAE *Operating Ratio Report*, the average association receives 41 percent of its revenues from dues; trade associations are more reliant on dues (which represent 46 percent of their revenues, on average) than individual membership organizations (36 percent, on average). In any case, dues revenue is too important to take for granted.

While individual membership organizations are likely to have a flat- or fixed-rate dues structure (70 percent favor this approach, according to *Policies & Procedures in Association Management*), only 26 percent of trade associations assess dues on that basis. Instead, corporate dues are usually related to some measure of size, volume, or wealth, such as total annual sales, number of employees, units of production, and so forth. The underlying assumption is that larger corporate members receive proportionally greater benefits from the association than do smaller members. Therefore, the single-store retailer ought to pay lower dues to the national organization than the chain retailer with multiple sites and a much larger budget. Some of these organizations have caps or maximum dues amounts for their largest members. This can present problems if the industry is consolidating: If a member paying maximum dues absorbs another member, the organization loses the latter's dues completely.

Any discussion of dues assessments brings up the issue of fairness, which, in turn, can greatly affect organizational politics. For instance, will the few large dues-paying members dominate the decision-making process? Should voting rights be proportional to dues paid? How far will the organization go to keep large companies as members, even if their needs are different from or contrary to the needs of many smaller members?

For example, the Health Insurance Agency of America (HIAA), of Washington, D.C., lost its four largest members—and hundreds of thousands of dollars in dues—when it opposed legislation favoring the managed care approach to healthcare. The four large companies and one that retained HIAA membership had already embraced the concept and formed a new association in support of managed care.

Multiple types of membership further complicate a dues discussion. If an organization has subordinate special interest groups, for example, it must decide whether membership in those groups is included in the "regular" dues or requires an additional fee. Like members of the industry or profession itself, suppliers may pay a flat fee to join the organization or be assessed dues on a sliding scale based on annual revenues. Defining the rights granted to these "associate" or "allied" members can be difficult, especially in trade associations that have vertical integration with suppliers, wholesalers, and retailers: Who votes? Who serves on which committees? Are they treated the same—or differently—than "buyer" members?

The Internal Revenue Service has muddied the waters further by questioning whether supplier dues are true membership assessments or mere payments for access to a market or buyers. Associations that have vendors as members should be able to explain how that category of membership furthers its nonprofit objectives.

Value for Dues Dollars

Rather than picking an amount out of the air, associations may base dues on what goods and services the member will receive in return. To keep dues lower, for example, an association may "unbundle" some goods and services from the basic dues package and ask members to pay separate fees to receive the extras.

That practice raises important questions: What do dues really purchase if the association prices and offers its most valuable goods and services separately? If most goods and services are fee-based, will membership in the association be like "membership" in for-profit organizations—like that of an American Express Card member? Does membership provide value in and of itself, or do dues represent an entry fee that provides access to other benefits? Such questions grow in significance in view of the *Policies and Procedures* finding that the proportion of association income spent on servicing members averages 51 percent.

Associations typically provide three types of benefits to members: advocacy; goods and services, including publications; and opportunities for volunteer involvement. Members assign varying value to these benefits, according to data published in *The Verdict: Professionals Evaluate Their Individual Membership Societies* and in *The Corporate View: How Business Executives Rate Their Trade Associations.* The two surveys indicated that most individuals join professional societies primarily for the information they receive from the association's publications. On the other hand, corporations believe that the most significant benefit of trade association membership involves presenting their industry's position to government.

But publications and advocacy aren't the only reasons for belonging. Also highly rated in both studies were developing professional contacts and meeting potential clients. It may be more difficult to put a price tag on these, but associations should look carefully at the perceived value of these more intangible benefits before deciding on a fee-based plan.

DATA-BASED VALUE TRACKING

One-to-one marketing has begun to evolve within associations. The Allegiance for Associations questionnaire allows individual members to identify their desired involvement. They can choose from eight categories.

- Mailboxer: "Just send me mail or e-mail."
- Relevant participant: "I'll come to meetings."
- Cognosenti: "Help me learn."
- Status Conscious: "Improve my image."
- Shaper: "Involve me in decision making."
- Altruistic: "I share your values, so let me give."
- Doubter: "Don't try anything new."
- Non-Relevant: "This really isn't for me anymore."

Categorizing members permits you to make intelligent decisions about the kinds of goods and services you promote to them and what you may ask of them. For example, you would not have to send elaborate promotional materials to people who are "non-relevants" because the odds of their enrollment in a program are low. On the other hand, mailing "relevant participants" a full promotion piece is cost-effective because their likelihood of program acceptance is high. For those organizations having difficulty recruiting volunteers, the self-identification of individuals as "shapers" helps them target recruitment efforts.

Using database technology, associations are increasingly able to identify members' individual needs and organize to meet them. Two out of three (66 percent) report that they track member participation in activities such as attending meetings, serving on a committee, and purchasing an association product or service.

Recruitment and Retention

Over the years, associations have learned that the best way to build membership numbers is to retain current members: It's less expensive to encourage people to renew their memberships than to attract new members. Associations report that the average tenure for membership is 13 years; they also report average attrition of 13 percent annually. By and large, the greatest turnover occurs during the early years of membership. This is the result of both unmet (or unrealistic) expectations and a desire for greater involvement.

To shape new members' expectations and to integrate them into activities, associations can undertake special communication efforts. These activities may include mailing a new-member kit immediately after receiving the application, making a follow-up call six months later to see how well the person's needs are being met, and recognizing new members at events so they feel comfortable and accepted. Another important retention tool is aggressive communication with recently lapsed members to determine the source of their discontent and explore ways to address those issues.

Some organizations strive to develop a "golden handcuff," a benefit so valuable that members feel compelled to remain in the association. This obviously eases concerns over recruitment and retention. But even a golden handcuff isn't foolproof: If an organization depends entirely on such a product, the danger always exists that a competing organization or for-profit business will duplicate the product and lure away members.

Most associations don't have a golden handcuff, but they do offer a wide range of activities, products, and services that their members view as valuable benefits. Why, then, doesn't everyone join? Why do some prospects fit the demographic profile of satisfied members yet refuse to join? You might think that part of the answer lies in demographic data, which aren't determinative. It's easy to believe that a prospect who resembles a current member is simply being ignorant by passing up the opportunity to join—but it's not true. If someone declines to join, there is a reason. What associations really need to ask the prospect is, "What would an association look like that you would want to join?" (See Chapter 6 on market research.)

A classic case arises in many a trade association that offers government relations and public relations activities as principal benefits of membership. Such services, which benefit the entire industry, trickle down to nonmembers for free. Consequently, when a recruiter pitches this valuable benefit of belonging, the potential member realizes that his or her company has already benefited from the association's representation without spending a dime. The prospect undoubtedly has needs the association could address, but advocacy isn't one of them. The trick is to find out how the needs of such prospects differ from those of current members and then decide whether it's worthwhile to attempt to meet those needs. And to discover what prospects and members want out of membership, associations must ask them.

Associations sometimes struggle with recruitment, not because of any inherent weakness in their lineup of products and services but because they approach prospects in the wrong way. In corporate membership organizations, for instance, dues are often relatively high. Therefore, direct, personal contact by senior officials of the organization would be the preferred recruitment technique.

On the other hand, individual membership organizations, such as the American Association of Retired Persons (AARP), of Washington, D.C., may charge only a nominal fee for membership, which gives the person access to a wide range of additional benefits that are priced separately. Because membership in such an organization isn't a major financial commitment, mass-market approaches, such as direct mail, generally prove more worthwhile than individualized contacts.

Growth Opportunities

Organizations occasionally consider reaching beyond their current demographic base to expand horizontally or vertically within the industry or profession. The New York Hotel/Motel Association, in Albany, for instance, decided to rename itself the New York Hospitality and Tourism Association. With the name change came an aggressive campaign to absorb other portions of the state's travel and tourism sector. Within one year, the association had attracted as members more than 75 amusement parks and attractions and about 100 bed-and-breakfast establishments.

The National Association of REALTORS® (NAR), of Chicago, which had traditionally catered to the owner-managers of brokerage firms, decided its best strategy for growth was to extend membership to individual sales agents. This strategy appeared highly successful at the outset but led to greater volatility in membership because many salespeople entered and exited the business as the real estate market expanded and contracted. Incorporating these new members into the association also changed the nature of NAR's governance system: The salespeople generally had little managerial or delegation experience so their expectations of staff and services differed markedly from those of the brokers.

Many national associations have begun to pursue an international orientation. The Society of Nuclear Medicine, of Reston, Virginia, for example, decided that rather than seeking to sign up part-time practitioners in the United States, it could best grow by building its relatively small base of international members.

Implementing a growth strategy generates additional issues. For instance, if advocacy is a major benefit of membership, should foreign members pay lower dues because they don't benefit from lobbying and representation in Washington? Or should they pay higher dues because it costs more to service international members? An association contemplating global expansion must grapple with whether it will be a domestically based organization that happens to allow members from around the world or a truly international organization.

Organizational Considerations

Both *The Corporate View* and *The Verdict* surveys found that members assigned a high perceived value to networking opportunities. The significance of that value, however, depended somewhat on the size and geographical distribution of the membership: The smaller and more geographically constrained the organization's membership, the greater the perceived benefits of networking.

WHAT'S IN A NAME?

There's more to expanding globally than putting the word "International" in front of an association's name, as the National Association of Amusement Parks discovered in 1972 when it became the International Association of Amusement Parks and Attractions (IAAPA). Initially, the association's newfound "global vision" was a mirage—it neither recruited members outside the United States nor translated materials for people whose first language wasn't English. Not surprisingly, few international members joined.

"The U.S. didn't invent the amusement park, but we took it to a whole new level. Park managers came from all over the world to see how things were done at Disney and other parks . . . . But by 1990, literally all the growth had gone overseas. Internationalization was absolutely crucial," recalls Susan Mosedale, vice president of membership and marketing at IAAPA, in Alexandria, Virginia.

IAAPA responded by creating its World Council, a group charged with making recommendations for association programming. The council has one representative from each of the nearly 80 countries with an IAAPA-affiliated park, and three of its members also serve on the IAAPA board of directors (one each from Europe, Latin America, and Asia). Once international members had gained a voice in governance, other activities changed rapidly. IAAPA prints its membership directory in five languages, offers videos in several languages other than English, and has translation services available at its annual trade show.

In 1995, it opened ten field offices around the world so members can receive assistance in their own time zones. Local amusement park associations provide the staff for each office (a few hours a week), while IAAPA pays for office expenses, such as postage and phone charges. Although it required a large initial investment, the program has grown less expensive over time, primarily because of the use of e-mail.

International members now represent 45 percent of IAAPA's core membership, which excludes vendors and suppliers. In 2000, the association reshaped the role of the World Council. Rather than serving as an advisory body to the association, it is now a group dedicated to networking and exchanging information among international members. "The World Council, which we refer to as the United Nations of amusement parks, had a value we didn't foresee when it was first formed," says Mosedale. "It is now a forum that facilitates discussion and enables members to learn from each other." Three seats on the IAAPA board are still designated for non-U.S. members, although the association anticipates phasing out that structure once its leadership development efforts draw more members from around the world.

Many associations, particularly individual membership organizations, use chapters as a primary recruitment tool. (This approach is certainly evident in service clubs, such as Rotary, Kiwanis, and Optimists International.) In general, chapter development also works well for trade associations with large numbers of potential members (such as boards of REALTORS® and chambers of commerce), as well as professional organizations, engineering societies, and so forth.

The chapter-based structure is a two-edged sword, however. A chapter can provide services at the local level more readily than could a national headquarters, but it also can have profound political consequences (see Chapter 2). Associations contemplating a chapter-based structure must consider whether membership will be integrated—that is, whether a member must belong to the national

CLOSING THE LOOP

In many trade associations with corporate members, a large number of employees in each corporation are either involved in association activities or personally enjoy the benefits of membership. Yet only one or two people in the corporation typically decide whether to join or remain a member, and those decision makers often derive less direct benefit from membership than do their subordinates.

The Envelope Manufacturers Association (EMA), of Alexandria, Virginia, closes the loop between the payment of dues and the value derived from them by tracking all contacts between a corporate member's employees and the association: obtaining answers to questions, purchasing goods, enrolling in education programs, attending conventions, and so forth. Along with the annual EMA dues invoice, decision makers receive a listing of all these contacts, plus a projected dollar value of such services. This information provides strong evidence of the real benefits of membership to whoever authorizes the membership renewal.

EMA also uses the information to reach out to members who derive little benefit from the organization. It generates a report showing how similar corporations are making the most of their association membership. Staff members sometimes make a presentation to employees of a relatively inactive corporation, showing how the association's resources can make an employee's job easier.

organization in order to belong to a state or local chapter. The alternative is empowering chapters to take on local members who have not joined at the national level. Either situation has significant potential for turf battles and competition for members between the parent organization and the chapters.

When they work cooperatively with national associations, chapters can profoundly affect recruitment at the local level. In fact, many organizations establish contests and rewards to encourage competition among chapters in the areas of recruitment and retention. Structured recruitment activities for local chapters may include "each one reach one" programs, direct mail campaigns, and phone-a-thons. In federations, of course, the chapters are the members. As an example, the members of the American Nurses Association, of Washington, D.C., are state nurses associations.

Almost every decision made by an association—from the amount of dues, to the services offered, to the structure of the organization itself—has some bearing on membership. Recruitment and retention efforts cannot be made in a vacuum; they must be integrated into the overall decision-making process so that every action is analyzed for its membership consequences. ■

Chapter

8

Publishing

Key Points

- Trade associations use publications to disseminate up-to-date industry statistics and legislative or regulatory information; professional societies use journals and magazines to keep members abreast of developments in the field.

- Market segmentation is the primary reason for the proliferation of periodicals: As organizations grow large enough to have significant subgroups within their membership, they must satisfy specialized needs for information.

- Given the explosive growth of electronic technology—and the advent of for-profit competitors—associations must become value-added repackagers and distributors of information.

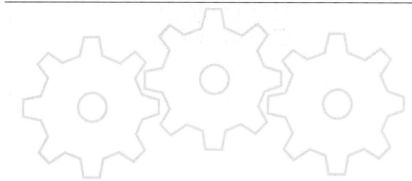

An irony of the association field is that members don't associate very much—not face-to-face, at any rate. But interaction and information exchange among members—a core benefit of most associations—occur in other ways, notably through the production and distribution of periodicals. Many associations find that their members rate publications as the number one benefit of belonging.

The vast majority of associations (95 percent) publish a periodical, such as a newsletter, magazine, or journal. In addition, two out of five (41 percent) publish books. In total, associations spend an estimated $5.6 billion annually on printing and publishing activities.

From the start, most associations provide a newsletter or other communication vehicle to foster interaction among members. Trade associations use publications to disseminate the up-to-date industry statistics and legislative or regulatory information that are other vital benefits of membership. Members of professional societies, though less advocacy-oriented, rely on journals and magazines to keep them abreast of developments in their field. Without this information, they risk obsolescence or irrelevance.

Some general-interest associations or affinity groups—the World Future Society and American Association of Retired Persons (AARP) to name just two—have such low dues that membership is equivalent to a subscription. As another example, people don't subscribe to *National Geographic*; they become members of the National Geographic Society, of Washington, D.C., and receive the magazine as a benefit of membership.

Types of Periodicals

The options for communicating in print range from newsletters and tabloid newspapers to technical or scientific journals, general-interest magazines, and bulletins and alerts. Most associations start with a newsletter and diversify their publications as membership grows.

Market segmentation is the primary reason for this proliferation of periodicals. As organizations grow large enough to have significant subgroups within their membership, they must satisfy specialized needs for information. Generally the first step is to allocate space for special-interest articles in the association's flagship publication. Eventually, however, many organizations provide special-interest groups with their own narrowly targeted publications in addition to the general magazine or journal. This second periodical often takes the form of a print or e-mail newsletter because production costs are relatively low—particularly when volunteers supply the content.

Most print newsletters appear monthly, run eight pages or fewer, and feature articles written by staff and volunteers. An e-mail newsletter might contain a synopsis of those same articles with links to the full text, which is posted on the association's Web site. Magazines—typically written by a mix of staff, volunteers, and paid contributors—can be as small as 24 pages or as large as 240 pages; they usually have specialized news departments as well as practical or "how to" articles. In contrast, journals focus on cutting-edge research and technical advances, with articles coming almost entirely from volunteers. (Journal articles typically are subjected to a volunteer peer-review process to ensure members of the quality of the research being presented.) Notices and alerts are generated almost exclusively by staff, based on information they accumulate in their daily work.

Contributors of Content

Each source of articles has advantages and disadvantages. Volunteers have an in-depth understanding of scientific, technical, and practical matters but may not be accomplished writers. Extensive editing by staff can make a piece useful and usable, but amateur writers may balk at accepting changes to their work. Too, a dependence on volunteer writers can wreak havoc with production schedules, especially for nontechnical publications that promise timely information. Volunteers often underestimate, or simply don't have, the time to write an article and may find it difficult to abide by deadlines.

Knowledgeable staff members can interview a number of people and produce balanced articles that reflect the association's diversity in terms of geography, gender, type of company, and so forth. For example, the Institute of Internal Auditors, of Altamonte Springs, Florida, relies on staff-written articles to present opinions of its many international members, who may not be proficient enough in English to submit a written article to *Internal Auditor* magazine but have little difficulty expressing themselves during a phone interview.

On the other hand, when staff members write all copy—or heavily edit member submissions—the publication may lose its distinctive voices because all articles sound alike. Turnover presents another problem. New staff members need time to get up to speed on the association's issues.

Cost can be a significant consideration as well. Smaller associations in particular usually can't afford to hire a full-time professional writer or editor. Associations that expect employees to wear a variety of hats may hire a competent meeting manager or advocate without giving any thought to the person's writing or editorial skills.

Freelancers offer excellent writing skills but probably lack knowledge in the arcane details of the trade or profession and may require several assignments to develop an expertise. Using freelancers also has implications for production schedules; magazines must increase their lead times to allow for editing and fact-checking. Some associations effectively blend the writing skills of one person and the expertise of another by hiring freelancers to "ghostwrite" columns or articles for volunteers.

Control and Competition

Magazines that function as "house organs" reflect the official position of the association and tend to emphasize news about members and organizational activities. Others have the editorial freedom to tackle controversial topics or take varied approaches to their content. At the American Bar Association, of Chicago, for example, the *ABA Journal* has the independence to operate without oversight by the board of directors. Backed by its volunteer editorial committee, the magazine has addressed political hot potatoes, such as the lack of women in ABA leadership positions.

The decision of editorial control has implications for the structure and management of the entire publishing effort. If a volunteer editor or editorial committee has general authority over publishing policies, subject to review by the entire board, can the volunteer board or senior staff compel the editor to publish or squelch certain information?

If so, leaders who exercise their veto power in an effort to avoid controversy may be contributing to a dull periodical with less appeal for readers as well as advertisers. This situation becomes particularly noticeable in fields where the for-profit trade press publishes more adventuresome periodicals that lure away readers and advertising dollars. But presenting alternative positions and addressing controversies through an association periodical certainly doesn't ease the difficult task of building consensus within the organization and presenting a unified front.

The vast majority of association periodicals are targeted at members, who typically receive the flagship publication as a part of their dues. Taking a tip from commercial competitors, some organizations have moved to "controlled circulation"—offering a publication free to people who "qualify" because they work in a particular field or industry. This can boost revenues by delivering a larger market to advertisers.

Production Issues

Mastering the nuts and bolts of production—which includes design, layout, typesetting, and printing—requires a knowledge base that most association executives lack. Therefore, while periodicals were traditionally written and edited in-house, associations entrusted most other facets of production to outside experts. Advances in technology have changed that approach. The introduction and growing popularity of desktop publishing, database management, electronic design, and illustration software programs have lowered the level of dependency on outside vendors.

The bad news is that some organizations believed that the mere purchase of publishing software packages gave their staffs the ability to create imaginative, pleasing layouts. That was rarely the case. The good news: After a few forays into in-house design that had negative consequences—such as lowering readership—many associations now either hire well-trained specialists in-house or contract with a professional to develop a design and then create templates to follow for individual layouts.

CHIPS OFF THE BLOCK

For more than 90 years, the American Library Association (ALA), of Chicago, had published a magazine of book reviews for its librarian members. In 1990, ALA reached beyond its traditional audience and launched a new publication for teachers who use children's books in their classrooms.

Book Links, the spin-off magazine, depends on the same staff, equipment, and expertise used to produce the association's flagship publication but repackages the specialized information in a classroom, rather than library, context. Its circulation is primarily to nonmembers of the association.

The American Academy of Family Physicians (AAFP), Leawood, Kansas, also launched a magazine in the early 1990s but directed its new product specifically at existing readers. Like AAFP's clinical journal, *Family Practice Management* goes to all members. But instead of taking a technical and scientific approach, the magazine focuses on the business of medicine—how to manage staff, apply for reimbursement, computerize an office, and so forth. The editorial staff gets much of its material from the academy's socioeconomics division, which gathers a lot of information but previously had no way of distributing it on a large scale.

Originally distributed with AAFP's scholarly journal, *Family Practice Management* now has an identity, personality, and distribution schedule of its own.

Developments in technology have improved other aspects of publishing as well. Bar-coded addresses get periodicals to readers in less time and for less money; ink-jet printing and selective binding technologies enable associations to produce personalized and customized publications that appeal to highly segmented memberships. Many now transmit copy electronically to printers, who then go directly from the computer file to the printing plate. Computer-to-plate (CTP) technology bypasses the need to make film, which decreases lead time and increases opportunities for editors to include timely or late-breaking information.

With printing representing a sizable portion of a publication's budget, contracts should be bid out regularly. *Association Publishing Procedures* indicates that a one- or two-year contract is the most common arrangement with printers. The contracts can cover much more than putting ink on paper. In some cases, they include typesetting, mailing, paper purchase and storage, or even technical editing. With so many dollars at stake, associations must have someone on staff who is well-versed in the minutiae of postage regulations, paper weight, type size, ink qualities, and so forth.

Different Delivery Methods

According to the ASAE *Operating Ratio Report*, printing/photocopying is the third largest expense area in associations (after personnel and meetings), representing 5.8 percent of total revenue. Given substantial printing costs and rising postage rates, associations have looked to alternate means of communicating with the members and other target audiences.

Associations have long been in the business of gathering and disseminating information. With the explosive growth of electronic technology—and the advent of for-profit competitors—they must now become value-added repackagers and distributors of information. That's the only way associations can continue to provide accurate, useful, and timely information to their members, whose very livelihood may depend on such intelligence.

For some associations, that has meant replacing printed and mailed newsletters with broadcast fax or fax-on-demand publications. Others have developed audiotapes and videotapes in magazine format or now publish detailed or archival information—such as directories, abstracts, and statistics—on CD-ROM. Still others post their membership directories, publication archives, and even some current articles on their Web sites. These items are typically in a members-only area accessible by member number or other type of password.

The Internet and World Wide Web also have opened new doors for associations wishing to improve or expand their services to members. At the Council for Advancement and Support of Education (CASE), of Washington, D.C., for example, several efforts to produce a newsletter advertising job opportunities didn't succeed, and the council's monthly magazine had too long a lead time for most interested job seekers and employers. But adding a job classifieds section to its Internet site did the trick for CASE, not only generating revenue for the organization but also giving members a reason to log on.

BORDER CROSSING

When the North American Free Trade Agreement (NAFTA) took effect, the National Retail Hardware Association (NRHA), of Indianapolis, Indiana, saw an opportunity for its members. By publishing a Spanish-language publication for readers in Mexico and Central and South America, the association could introduce its members' products—hardware and building materials—to a new market that was experiencing rapid growth in home-improvement retailing.

NRHA discovered that simply translating its flagship publication into Spanish wouldn't work—the magazine offers how-to management information, while the new markets wanted product information. So *Productos Nuevos,* which contains articles on new products and merchandising trends, was born in early 1995. Although launching the tabloid required much research into translation services and international delivery methods, the association has built the controlled circulation of *Productos Nuevos* to more than 20,000 readers and publishes it three times per year.

Associations often use their Internet sites or "home pages" to disseminate information to members as well as consumers; conduct surveys; sign up members; and handle registration for or sales of upcoming seminars, publications, or events. Some use their print publications to drive traffic to a Web site, where the association may post a longer version of an article, additional charts and graphs, or other material that did not fit the space constraints of a printed piece.

Like any other medium, an Internet Web site should offer useful, timely, accurate, and significant information that's updated regularly. That means charging some staff with the responsibility of maintaining the site's vitality and relevance—no minor challenge, because regular online users are accustomed to daily or even hourly updates.

Many associations also use the capacity of the Internet for the hosting of chat rooms or listservers so that subgroups of members can have a focused forum for idea exchange and networking.

Despite the growing popularity of electronic communications, publishing experts predict the need for printed journals and magazines won't diminish. After all, they argue, television didn't replace radio or motion pictures but augmented people's choices for information and entertainment. Likewise, associations need to expand their publishing offerings to appeal to members' varied appetites for information. ∎

Education and Meetings

Key Points

- Without both formal and informal research, assessing the crowd appeal of educational meetings is a hit-and-miss proposition.

- Logistical decisions depend not only on a meeting's purpose but also on the nature of the attendees, their price sensitivity, and the association's available resources.

- Whether planning a traditional meeting or an electronic one, an effective meeting planner must be a detail-oriented negotiator, problem solver, and communicator.

No matter how high its quality and how valuable its content, a publication cannot take the place of face-to-face meetings in bringing members together. In addition, effectively planned and executed meetings are crucial to all parts of the governance structure, including boards of trustees, boards of directors, houses of delegates, and all manner of committees (budget and finance, public policy, program, publications, and so forth). Thanks to technology, however, electronic meetings are being convened more and more for both governance and educational purposes.

Association Meeting Trends (1999) notes that the average association plans one convention/annual meeting, one exposition, nine educational seminars, and four board/executive meetings each year. Some meetings are held in conjunction with others; 63 percent of associations schedule an exposition together with their annual meeting.

These meetings can mean big business: The fees generated by conventions, educational programs, and exhibits represent the largest category of nondues income—nearly 26 percent of total revenue for the average association. And, in total, associations spend $56 billion annually to hold conventions, meetings, and expositions.

Traditional Meetings

An average of 37 percent of associations' members attend meetings each year. They may be motivated by a desire to learn, share, debate, make decisions, network, or simply socialize, and different types of meetings address these various needs.

Conventions/annual meetings are usually multi-day events. In a single-track convention, everyone essentially does the same thing at the same time. A typical convention schedule might include a social breakfast followed by an educational program, luncheon speech, concurrent business sessions for various committees, and social events in the evening.

Larger events often feature "tracks" designed for subsets of members. A series of programs, for example, may be designed for people new to the field or for specialists in a particular area. These educational tracks usually operate simultaneously, in addition to general sessions, committee meetings, and social events interspersed throughout the convention.

Looking beyond their members, more than half of associations (58 percent) offer guest or spouse programs at their conventions; 17 percent offer children's programs. The most popular sites for these large meetings are city hotels, resorts, and convention centers.

Educational programs/seminars, although usually included as part of a convention, also operate as stand-alone meetings. State, national, and international associations are increasingly using distance learning to provide more convenient and accessible learning opportunities to their far-flung membership. Both trade associations and individual membership organizations typically favor city hotels as sites for educational seminars.

Expositions/trade shows usually offer association members the chance to browse displays of the latest goods and services offered by various suppliers. Some supplier associations hold trade shows for their customers. The Automotive Trade Association of the Greater Washington (D.C.) Area organizes events in which its members display their own goods and services to the public.

Determining Content

The educational content of a ball-bearing trade association's annual meeting will clearly differ from a convention sponsored by a medical society. But one rule applies to both: Attracting participants requires marketing.

Marketing starts with gaining an understanding of the self-perceived educational needs of the market (see Chapter 6). This may be accomplished by conducting formal surveys through publications or direct mail. Less formal research methods include focus groups, ad hoc committees composed of association members, and attendance figures from previous seminars on similar topics. Without these kinds of research, the crowd appeal of educational meetings is a hit-and-miss proposition.

The next task is to decide who will present the information—and how. In most organizations, the program committee—or whoever is responsible for determining educational content—identifies and invites speakers with recognized expertise in the desired subject. Presenters may be either association members or outside experts. Nearly three out of four associations (71 percent) pay professional speakers or celebrities to speak at their conventions; one out of two (50 percent) pays for the same talent for educational seminars.

Technical or scientific societies may stray a bit from this market-driven approach because they thrive on up-to-the-minute research in narrow or arcane fields. Asking members what they want to know won't help in planning—they're probably unaware of the latest discovery or advance. Instead, members involved in research submit proposals to a program committee, which oversees a peer-review process that selects papers for presentation.

For professionals in the fields of academia or research, having a paper selected for presentation is a significant honor that receives much attention from promotion and tenure committees. As a result, the competition for presentation slots can be intense. The Society of Nuclear Medicine, for example, solicits its 13,000 members for abstracts to be presented at the annual scientific meeting. In recent years, the society has received more than 2,000 abstracts per year. The peer-review committee selects less than 25 percent of these for presentation. Papers of secondary interest or importance may be offered a slot in a "poster session," which permits the participant to prepare written materials and graphics to display on bulletin boards set up in a separate room at the meeting.

Logistics

Even before conducting research or soliciting abstracts, an association must settle a more basic issue: the purpose of the meeting. Is it to be purely educational, or will it provide an opportunity for networking as well?

GETTING STARTED

Answering the following questions can narrow the many logistical choices available and lead to a meeting that suits members' needs as well as the association's budget:

- What is the meeting intended to accomplish?

- Where are most participants located? Is it necessary or advisable to rotate the meeting among several regions or cities?

- Is the group recreation- or sports-oriented or more likely to favor nightlife and sightseeing? Would participants prefer an urban site, a resort, or a conference center?

- Are spouses and families likely to accompany the participants? Should the meeting serve as a jumping-off point for pre- and post-convention trips?

- Does anyone in the group require special accommodations because of physical disability?

- What kind of accommodations can participants afford? Would they prefer a prestigious property or something more modest?

Source: The Convention Liaison Council Manual, *6th Edition.*

The numerous logistical decisions related to a meeting—from site selection to catering to entertainment—depend not only on the meeting's purpose but also on the nature of the attendees, their price sensitivity, and the association's available resources. That's why it's unlikely that the American Student Nurses Association would meet at the same location as the Motion Picture Association of America. Image is another consideration. After years of holding its winter meeting at a Florida resort, one national organization instead opted for urban hotels in cities with high concentrations of its members; leaders believed that continuing to meet at a beachfront property didn't fit the group's activist image.

Even with a firm grasp of these issues, a meeting planner faces a dizzying selection of options. They include but aren't limited to:

- Type of facility. Hotels typically come to mind first, and they represent the majority of meeting facilities used by associations. The key is to select a site that matches the meeting's goals: efficiency, congeniality, a balance of work and leisure activities, and so forth. For instance, using an airport hotel can emphasize convenience, especially if most attendees will arrive by air. A meeting at a downtown property might compete with shopping, museums, and sightseeing, compared with a suburban hotel where members are more likely to stick together and attend the program.

  Alternatives to hotels include conference centers, convention centers, and even college campuses, which are often available for rent. Local groups with limited budgets might locate meeting space at shopping centers, banks, churches, or synagogues.

- Layout. Again, the meeting's purpose—not the type of facility—should dictate how rooms are set up. An auditorium style (rows of seats facing a dais) might make the most sense if you're pinched for space, but that choice probably won't encourage much interaction among attendees. A classroom-style arrangement with cloth-covered tables looks professional but can use up a lot of space—certainly a consideration if a large group is expected. If tables are provided—which encourage people to take notes and consume refreshments—will they be lined up in straight rows, angled to form a chevron, or arranged into a hollow U or a hollow circle? Or should the tables be round to encourage small group breakout activities during the educational program?

- Resources. In addition to microphones, speakers may want slide projectors, overhead projectors, direct video-projection systems, videocassette recorders, or computer equipment and access lines.

- Catering. According to *Association Meeting Trends*, associations typically include four meals in an annual meeting registration fee, which might range from a sit-down dinner to a breakfast buffet to an hors d'ouevres reception. Choices will depend on the budget and what members expect. Other considerations: How health conscious are members? Can the facility accommodate requests for vegetarian, low-sodium, no MSG, kosher, and other special diets?

- Multiple sites. Large-scale events that use space at more than one site generally require a bus or shuttle service between locations to ensure participants have access to all activities. Some groups also offer ground transportation to and from the airport.

- Outside help. Although three out of five associations (61 percent) have a full-time staff dedicated to meeting planning, staff members can't do everything themselves. Outside contractors can help with details ranging from providing security to lining up entertainment.

- Americans with Disabilities Act. This law requires meeting managers to make "reasonable accommodations" to meet the needs of attendees who are disabled. Most meeting reservation forms solicit information about such needs in advance.

With so many considerations, a meeting manager must be able to think through all the elements involved in an effective convention or seminar and anticipate possible glitches and complications. He or she must be able to communicate those details to the staffs of both the association and the hotel through master schedules, reports, and checklists. In addition, the meeting manager should be an effective negotiator and problem solver who, despite a natural obsession with details, can respond flexibly and maturely when a crisis occurs.

Of course, all of this takes place in view of the budget, what the meeting is intended to accomplish, who the participants are, and what attendees want to experience. Creativity lies in developing a new format or approach to achieving the meeting's and the members' goals.

Electronic Meetings

Associations are increasing their use of electronic means for both governance meetings and for education and training. Telephone conference calls have been used for some time for committee meetings when time is short and the issues are few. While some associations are using the Internet to discuss and make decisions, many states have laws that don't permit asynchronous decision making by boards (though this is changing). (Asynchronous refers to meetings where participants don't have the opportunity to interact simultaneously.) Committee work, on the other hand, can be legally transacted in any practical way. A number of techniques can be used over the Internet to provide support for group decision making, such as a listserver, live chat, or secure Web site.

The use of electronic media for educational purposes isn't new. Although the logistics are expensive and a bit complicated, satellite transmission of education has been used for some time. Too, audiotapes, videotapes, and audioconferences have been around for a while. The capacity of CD-ROMs has permitted interactive programmed learning.

The explosion of the Internet and the increasing availability of adequate bandwidth have increased the use of both synchronous and asynchronous education and training, with more growth likely as fiber optics, DSL, cable modems, and other broadband facilities become more widespread. Some organizations, for example, are Web-casting key sessions from their annual meeting and archiving them so that members who are unable to attend in person can still receive the benefit of the programs. Others offer a "virtual" version of their trade show or exposition, which enables members to visit exhibitors on a Web site for several months after the actual show has ended.

Even so, face-to-face meetings probably won't go the way of the slide rule and 8-track tape player. Large group activities provide an unusual opportunity for networking and "hallway learning" that electronic means cannot duplicate. The serendipity of contact and conversation is one of the most significant benefits of the large group get-together. The challenge for associations will be to compete with the for-profit firms that spring up to offer education to their members. ■

Voluntary Standards

Key Points

- Standards set by associations touch nearly every facet of life, from building codes to product safety guidelines to professional codes of ethics.

- In contrast to licensure and registration, certification is administered by private bodies, usually trade and professional associations.

- Accreditation is to institutions what certification is to individuals.

Regulating the conduct of an industry or profession would seem to be one of the most popular and accepted activities in which an association could engage. After all, who could be against setting technical standards to make products safer? Who would object to practitioners in a field earning a credential that recognizes their mastery of specific skills?

Yet such activities may raise eyebrows at the Justice Department and the Federal Trade Commission, which zealously enforce the provisions of the Sherman Act and other antitrust laws. They aim to ensure, for instance, that adhering to a code of ethics doesn't lead to price collusion or inhibit a professional from finding employment unless he or she has obtained certification from an association.

Although all four types of standards discussed below have fallen afoul of antitrust laws at times, a carefully crafted set of standards can benefit both the competition and the consumer.

Codes of Ethics

Slightly more than one out of two associations surveyed for *Policies and Procedures in Association Management* have a code of ethics that governs the conduct of its members. Furthermore, the majority of those associations (70 percent) make the code mandatory—a member must subscribe to the code to obtain or retain membership.

Ethical codes can range from a set of guidelines for behavior—often handsomely framed, prominently displayed, and otherwise ignored—to strict policies that spell out what actions are or aren't acceptable in the eyes of the association. Enforcement varies as well, with only one out of three associations reporting that it has methods of enforcing a code of ethics. Penalties for violation may range from a written, confidential reprimand to expulsion from the organization. In rare cases where state enforcement takes place—when the association and the licensing and regulatory arms of state government are "integrated," as in some state bar associations—the practitioner's license may be revoked and he or she may be suspended or even expelled from the profession.

Once widespread, strict enforcement of ethical codes began to wane in the 1970s. That's when practitioners in several professions successfully challenged in court their associations' ethical provisions limiting their right to advertise. Interestingly, some professional associations that provide peer review for the ethics of their members' work have enforced compliance. The California Dental Association, of Sacramento, for instance, enforces quality-related peer-review decisions through a code of ethics with which members must comply. The peer-review committee might require the member to attend certain types of continuing education programs to upgrade his or her skills in specific practice areas.

Still, any organization contemplating an enforceable ethical code should set aside a considerable sum for both the enforcement proceedings and the legal challenges that will inevitably arise.

Technical Standards

Technical standards fall into two broad categories: design and performance. Design standards outline specific materials to be used and the dimensions of the finished product. Performance standards deal with how the finished product should work, rather than how it is designed or manufactured.

Standards set by associations touch nearly every facet of life. Take, for example, the American Standard Code for Information Interchange (ASCII). It established a base set of characters and formatting tools that enable personal computers made by different companies to communicate with one another. Or the Fire Protection Code, established by the National Fire Protection Association, of Quincy, Massachusetts, and incorporated into many municipal ordinances that govern the construction of buildings. Or Generally Accepted Accounting Principles (GAAP), set by the Financial Accounting Standards Board and adhered to by commercial and nonprofit organizations alike.

In other countries, the government takes the lead in determining technical standards. But in the United States, standards set by associations and private-sector organizations typically develop first and then may find their way into official government codes. Because associations undertake the work voluntarily—not only to enhance their members' image but also to ensure their members' continued livelihood—taxpayers don't foot the bill. In fact, the American Society of Association Executives estimates that American associations spend 400 times more than the government on setting and enforcing product and safety standards.

Typically, an association convenes groups of interested and knowledgeable parties to work out the details of these standards. All parties should receive reasonable notice before standards are finalized and have opportunities to participate in the decision process. In addition, anyone affected by the standards should have avenues for appeal if they disagree with the final product.

CERTIFIABLE SUCCESS

In the late 1970s, as certification programs began to flourish in allied health professions, such as medical technologists and athletic trainers, a group of nonprofits organized the National Council of Health Certifying Agencies (NCHCA) to foster consistent testing guidelines. In 1989, NCHCA cast its net still wider to include professions outside the health field and evolved into the National Organization for Competency Assurance (NOCA).

The Washington, D.C.-based NOCA has established a set of criteria against which to measure certification programs. The basic steps for obtaining NOCA approval include:

1. An analysis that determines the crucial body of knowledge that someone must master to successfully accomplish a specified task.
2. Development of a syllabus or curriculum that covers the body of knowledge.
3. Development of a test to measure one's mastery of the material.
4. A series of validations of the testing instrument.
5. Adequate provisions for test administration and security.
6. A well-supported justification for the cut-off point—the point above which applicants pass the examination and below which they fail.

An association's work doesn't end with the publishing of the technical standards. The National Fire Protection Association, for example, provides technical support for individuals who have questions concerning the interpretation and application of its codes. Many associations' work, in turn, is validated by one of two umbrella organizations for standard setting: the American National Standards Institute (ANSI) and the American Society for Testing and Materials (ASTM). These two organizations qualify other associations to act as "secretariats" or supervising entities; essentially, ANSI and ASTM set the standards for the standard setters.

As business and industry have become increasingly global, U.S. associations have deepened their involvement in the establishment of international standards (through ISO, the International Standards Organization) or regional standards (for instance, the European Common Market).

Certification

Licensure generally refers to meeting standards set by or involving a state or other governmental body—such as a licensed practical nurse who has fulfilled certain state requirements for training and limits himself or herself to state-approved activities on the job. Registration, also undertaken by state authorities, is usually less rigorous than licensure. It doesn't necessarily require educational or performance prerequisites. A registered lobbyist, for example, may not have minimum criteria to meet.

In contrast, *certification* is administered by private bodies, usually trade and professional associations. Physicians, for example, are licensed to practice by the state but may also be certified in a specialized area, such as family medicine or radiology, based on tests given by the specialty's professional society or certification board.

Although medical societies pioneered certification programs, the practice has spread to include professions as diverse as financial planning, counseling, automotive servicing, meeting planning, and even association management. Typically, certification requires applicants to meet certain criteria regarding experience and education and to pass an examination. Many organizations also require recertification every three or five years, usually through continuing education.

A few associations grant certification to people who merely attend a series of courses. Although this may please members by making the credential easily obtainable, it will have little or no meaning to outside professionals who are aware of the typically rigorous certification process. In contrast, a well-constructed and well-promoted certification program adds luster to both individual practitioners and to the profession as a whole. Certified practitioners gain a competitive advantage over their colleagues who don't seek the credential, and the entire field benefits markedly as the quality of individual practitioners begins to rise.

Despite these advantages, creating a new certification program can cause controversy. One issue to resolve early on is how to handle current members: Will there be a provision to "grandfather in" senior practitioners, or will everyone have to follow the same path to certification? Some associations have addressed this issue by allowing current members to complete a personal data form to verify their experience in the field or to sit for qualifying examinations without attending the seminars required of newcomers.

Accreditation

Accreditation is to institutions what certification is to individuals. Just as a physician is licensed by the state and certified by a specialty medical group, so a hospital receives its license from the state and is reviewed by the Joint Commission for the Accreditation of Healthcare Organizations, a private accrediting body.

Colleges and universities are also frequently subject to review by regional accrediting agencies. Furthermore, accreditation boards of relevant specialty societies, such as the National Association of Schools of Public Administration, may examine individual programs or departments within a college or university.

While certification usually depends on an individual's mastery of a body of knowledge, accreditation programs test an institution's ability to do its job effectively. Therefore, accreditation tends to involve self-administered questionnaires that compare a facility to operational benchmarks. These questionnaires frequently are supplemented by site visits of examiners from the accrediting body, who seek to verify the institution's compliance with established criteria.

A QUESTION OF IDENTITY

When the Art Directors Club of Metropolitan Washington (ADCMW), Washington, D.C., looked at the graphic design industry, it saw no recognized educational requirements, no core competencies, no standard practices in billing, and no ethical code. The organization identified certification as an effective way to redefine and reestablish the identity of a profession being buffeted by technological developments, such as computerized illustration.

ADCMW scheduled a roundtable discussion on the topic and invited representatives of other professions offering certification, such as interior design and public relations. A survey conducted before the meeting revealed that 45 percent already favored certification; 11 percent were opposed; and the remaining 44 percent were undecided.

A funny thing happened on the way to the forum, however. After hearing the praises of certification sung by members of other creative professions, the proportion of those in favor edged up to 46 percent. On the other hand, the group opposed to certification more than doubled to 27 percent. Why? The members felt that design was too subjective a field for a certification panel to make judgments about.

The results prompted ADCMW to table certification—at least until members become convinced that the credential would apply to their professional qualifications, not their artistic abilities.

Ins and Outs

Associations engage in standard-setting activities to encourage and recognize quality. As worthy as it is, this goal can generate controversy, particularly in the areas of certification and accreditation. Some in the organization will argue that only the best programs or practitioners deserve recognition; those at the other extreme see certification or accreditation as a baseline or minimum standard, rather than as an exclusive club.

Complicating this debate is the fact that quality can be measured by at least two standards: inputs and outcomes. For example, the Joint Commission for the Accreditation of Healthcare Organizations (JCAHO) has historically measured an institution's potential for producing quality. It looked at factors such as the credentials of professional staff, availability of high-tech equipment, and establishment of certain internal processes. Increasingly, however, JCAHO is looking at whether institutions actually produce quality outcomes.

Determining such measures provokes some controversy: Is it possible to use the same standards to measure two healthcare institutions with different patient mixes? Likewise, how might outcome measurements replace accreditation standards for colleges and universities—would one measure the economic success of graduates or whether they had developed a greater appreciation for literature, art, or the world in general?

Given this debate, it's useful to keep the value of certification and accreditation programs in perspective: They are merely goals, not guarantees. A well-designed standard-setting program will encourage the ambitious to strive for higher quality—a worthy goal, even if its achievement can never be measured in absolute terms.

Most accreditation programs require reaccreditation on some regular basis; however, many certification programs do not. The issue of how to assure continued competence of certified individuals is a difficult one for many associations. ■

Research and Statistics

- Two out of five associations conduct research or gather data on their members' profession or industry.

- Some associations use the data they collect to improve the image of their trade or profession among the wider public.

- The most useful surveys are conducted regularly, allowing members not simply a "snapshot" of their industry or profession but rather a panoramic view of where they've been and where they're headed.

Mention statistics to most people, and their first reaction is a yawn. Mention the price that businesses are willing to pay for those statistics, and the yawn turns to a gulp. Seven out of ten associations (71 percent) conduct research or gather data on their members' profession or industry, and businesses and government rely heavily on that economic, demographic, social, or industrial information.

A glance at studies conducted in just one industry reveals the scope and variety of statistics available. For instance, the Food Institute, based in Fairlawn, New Jersey, has reported that Americans spend about $200 billion per year eating and drinking in commercial restaurants. In its annual Food Retailing Review, the institute noted that the average American spends $1,620 per year on food outside the home and that the average person in Honolulu spends $5,634 a year cooking at home, compared with $4,123 in Detroit.

Anyone in the highly competitive food industry would find such information invaluable. Accordingly, it doesn't come cheap: $195 for Food Institute members, $495 for nonmembers. Even at the nonmember price, the information represents a bargain compared with some privately conducted research studies. One 435-page report packed with statistics from the processed meat industry sold for $1,095, and a 204-page study titled *The Market for Coffee and Tea* went for $1,750. Both were produced by New York consulting firms.

Types of Studies

Faced with competition from the private sector, many associations are under pressure to produce research that gives their members even more reasons to belong. These studies, undertaken in addition to market research activities (see Chapter 6), may take many forms.

■ Industry- or profession-specific studies are the most popular according to *Policies & Procedures in Association Management.* Conducted by two out of five associations (41 percent), these focus on particular issues or areas of interest to members. The National Association of Home Builders, of Washington, D.C., for example, tracks the number of housing starts each month.

- Compensation surveys, conducted by 41 percent of associations that engage in industry research, enable employers to compare the salaries they offer with state, regional, or national averages.
- Market studies, often produced by trade associations, assess the characteristics of a marketplace, such as consumer demographics, potential sales volume, and average prices. Helpful in creating new products or entering new markets, these studies require great care on the part of the sponsoring association and benefit from consultation with legal counsel. Information must be gathered in such a way that it isn't construed as collusion or price fixing, which would run afoul of antitrust laws.
- Benchmarking studies, an outgrowth of the total quality management movement, seek out and identify the "best practice" in a given area so others can learn from and emulate it.
- Operating ratios compare sources of income and expenses, allowing members to assess how their operations fare against organizations of comparable size, scope, and type.

Factors to Consider

Industry data that are not available elsewhere can be a vital product for binding members to their organization. Some associations go a step further and use the data they collect to improve the image of their trade or profession among the wider public. For example, the National Association of Purchasing Management, in Tempe, Arizona, publishes a monthly report on industrial purchases that regularly receives coverage in the *Wall Street Journal* because it's considered an important economic indicator. Likewise, the American Association of Fund Raising Counsel, of New York City, publishes an annual report on the state of philanthropy that receives widespread recognition throughout the nonprofit sector and in the national media.

With the potential of additional audiences in mind, one question to ask before beginning a research project is: Who will be interested in the information? After identifying the audience, the association must decide who is best suited to collect the information. Because the majority of associations (73 percent) that conduct industry research don't employ a full-time research staff, it's common to seek outside expertise to ensure credibility, statistical accuracy, and confidentiality. Even those that have such talent in-house often turn to outside suppliers to collect sensitive information, such as sales and salary data. Members may be reluctant to release proprietary information unless the survey's confidentiality is ensured.

Another resource, often overlooked, is a local college or university. Professors and graduate students often take on significant research projects as part of their work on individual theses and dissertations. They can help an association keep its costs low and research quality high.

The most useful surveys are conducted regularly—perhaps every two to five years—allowing members not simply a "snapshot" of their industry or profession but rather a panoramic view of where they've been and where they're headed. To obtain such trend data, researchers must think beyond immediate needs to anticipate the kind of information members will need in the future.

A survey's validity and usefulness increase with its response rate. If too few people respond, projecting the results onto a larger universe of members becomes questionable. To encourage cooperation, organizations offer an array of incentives, the most popular of which is a free or deeply discounted copy of the survey results. Because most members understand that survey development is an expensive proposition and the information produced is vital to sound business decisions, this carrot has proved especially effective.

The effort required to provide requested information also affects response rates. The extent to which members are asked to report data that they do not collect in the ordinary course of business is inversely related to their willingness to participate. In other words, the more work you ask people to do, the less likely they are to do it. Consequently, researchers must understand the types of data that targeted participants already collect and can access easily.

Funding Sources

Few associations—approximately one out of ten—look on industry research as a profit center. Most prefer to conduct such activities as a benefit to members. Some groups ensure their costs are covered up front by assessing those members who are interested in seeing the outcome of the research. Others price findings on the basis of value rather than cost, opening the door to greater potential profits.

Foundations, which raise their own funds, may express interest in underwriting a specific association research project or providing a grant. Because foundations may prefer to give to other 501(c)(3) organizations, 501(c)(6) associations, before seeking foundation support, sometimes create their own (c)(3) organization to receive the funds and perform the research. The California Dental Association Foundation, based in Sacramento, for example, received about $400,000 from the deep-pocketed Kellogg Foundation to research techniques for evaluating ambulatory dental care.

The federal government also provides financial support for research projects it considers to be in the public interest. This largesse, however, comes with strings attached. Federal grant and contract recipients are subject to a wide range of limitations on their activities outside the specific research project. Therefore, association executives thinking about pursuing federal grants should first become familiar with the trade-offs inherent in such activities. ■

Suppliers as a Market

Key Points

- Suppliers are a lucrative part of the membership mix and can generate revenues through exhibit fees, sponsorships, and advertising.

- In associations where suppliers provide a substantial portion of the revenue stream, supplier members tend to be sought out and integrated into the organizational structure.

- When and if the interests of the core members and the supplier community diverge, the association should side with the core members and pursue their interests with all available resources.

A group of people involved in the same industry or profession represents a dream come true for suppliers to that field. In turn, those suppliers are a dream come true for association marketers, who see them as an important—and lucrative—part of the membership mix. For while the average association receives less than 2 percent of its income from suppliers' membership dues, it can generate a greater percentage from exhibit fees, sponsorships, and advertising.

Opportunities for Involvement

Some associations have become vertically integrated. In other words, their membership includes suppliers, middlemen, and end-users of a particular product or technology. For instance, Meeting Professionals International (MPI), based in Dallas, enrolls both meeting planners and suppliers (hotels, airlines, and so forth) as full members. The Aluminum Association, in Washington, D.C., while made up of manufacturers, also includes in its core membership the aluminum fabricators who are the manufacturers' primary customers. (A secondary membership category exists for the ultimate consumers of aluminum products.)

Most associations aren't so thoroughly integrated. *Policies & Procedures in Association Management* reports that one out of two associations doesn't have a membership category for industry vendors. Of those that do, the majority (68 percent) offer their "associate" or "affiliate" members different benefits than primary members.

Of course, some associations question whether to open membership to suppliers at all. But if the association's primary members represent a valuable market, including suppliers as members can add to the success of many activities.

TRADE SHOWS

A trade show can be as simple as a few tabletop exhibits in a hotel meeting room in Peoria or as extensive as Pack Expo (sponsored by the Packaging Machinery Manufacturers Institute, of Washington, D.C.), which uses more than 900,000 square feet of exhibit space at Chicago's McCormick Place and attracts about 85,000 attendees. Trade shows give members the opportunity, at no cost to them, to "kick the tires" on products and keep up with the latest developments in their industry or profession. At large medical equipment shows, for example, like the one mounted by the Radiological Society of North America, of Oak Brook, Illinois, attendees not only talk to salespeople but also watch demonstrations and see the equipment in action.

Even if suppliers contributed nothing to an association but active participation in its trade show, the financial payoff would be worthwhile. Convention center rental rates tend to be inexpensive compared with the prices charged exhibitors for booth space. Moreover, most of the work is done by decorating companies that provide move-in/move-out coordination, construction, design, and various other services that exhibitors pay for. To the association falls the job of delivering a critical mass of buyers to make the show valuable for exhibitors—usually not a problem because trade shows are often held in conjunction with annual meetings or educational programs.

In view of the lucrative nature of trade shows, commercial enterprises have cropped up in many industries to compete with associations for exhibitors as well as attendees. In response, some associations have adopted an "if you can't beat 'em, join 'em" approach, integrating their activities with a for-profit trade show and sharing revenues with a show's provider or promoter. As an example, the Electronic Industries Association, in Washington, D.C., formed a partnership with the corporation that owns COMDEX, the largest trade show in the United States. Likewise, the International Association for Exposition Management, of Dallas, Texas, outsources its show to a management firm and shares the profits.

Another recent development is the omnibus trade show in which several groups that share a common interest—such as purchasing the same goods and services—schedule their educational programs for the same time and location. Combined, all their members provide the attendance necessary for a successful trade show. This has proven successful for the 19 sporting goods associations that jointly hold "The Super Show" each year and attract about 110,000 attendees. In the manufacturing arena, 24 trade shows take place simultaneously during National Manufacturing Week; paying one registration fee enables an attendee to attend all the shows.

Many associations create a trade show advisory committee with representatives from both the buyer and seller communities. The committee typically advises on issues such as booth height, setback, noise regulations, and guidelines for demonstrations. It may also address questions such as: Will the show be open to interested parties outside the association's membership to boost attendance? If so, on what terms (higher price, limited times, and so forth)?

Such committees prove particularly helpful when suppliers aren't eligible for membership, because they provide opportunities for interaction and feedback between buyers and sellers. In addition, exhibitors are more likely to comply with trade show rules they've helped develop.

To maintain the integrity of their trade shows, most associations mail a prospectus that amounts to a request for proposal from potential exhibitors. Suppliers must state their business and apply for exhibit space, but the contract isn't complete until ratified by the association. This ensures that only appropriate exhibitors—those that meet the business or professional needs of the core membership—participate in the show. Such a rule would, for example, exclude a housewares manufacturer from the exhibit hall of a medical society.

Sometimes trade show roles are reversed, with supplier associations staging the show as a means of promoting their products and services to consumers or other buyers who aren't members. Marketing such shows is more problematic and expensive than those sponsored by associations of buyers, where the audience is discrete, well-defined, and easy to reach.

Some associations extend the reach of their trade show by mounting a virtual trade show on the Internet. Often, these consist of exhibitor listings on the association's Web site with some basic information and hot links to each vendor's Web page.

ADVERTISING

Association publications offer suppliers the opportunity to regularly and repeatedly reach members—who don't necessarily attend trade shows—with sales messages. When evaluating advertising opportunities, companies typically evaluate the CPM (cost per 1,000 readers) as well as the type of person being reached (reviewer, final decision maker, and so forth). Standard Rate and Data Service (SRDS), which compiles and publishes the advertising rates of many publications, offers a helpful picture of what other associations—and their commercial competitors—charge suppliers for access to readers. Advertising rates will vary with location within the publication, size, use of color, and frequency of placement.

Increasingly, associations are accepting Web site advertising, which may range from classified listings to banner ads to sponsorship of specific content areas. The Internal Revenue Service (IRS) considers advertising sales to be unrelated business income and therefore subject to taxation. In addition, accepting advertising can affect postage costs for associations wishing to take advantage of nonprofit mailing rates. The IRS is reviewing how, if at all, unrelated business income tax would apply to sponsorship of Web sites.

SPONSORSHIPS

Associations frequently look to suppliers to foot the bill for specific events or activities. Medical societies, for instance, often turn to pharmaceutical companies to cover the costs of speaker transportation and honoraria at educational programs. Some of the more creative associations have landed sponsors for everything from bus transportation to coffee breaks at their annual meetings. Others offer "sponsorship packages" that, for a flat fee, give suppliers exhibit space, recognition at a meeting, and perhaps a discounted ad in the association publication.

In return, suppliers can use sponsorships to build name recognition and generate goodwill among members by supporting the association's activities. The IRS has been working to define the line between sponsorship and advertising. Though there are exceptions, associations are generally able to publicize a sponsor's name and logo in connection with a sponsored event without having the IRS call it advertising. But associations should not list qualitative information regarding the sponsor (e.g., "lowest price," "high quality," etc.) if they wish to avoid having the payment treated as taxable advertising income. Associations thinking about sponsorships should get up-to-date information on how to structure the agreement in light of evolving tax rules and regulations.

ENDORSED PROGRAMS AND ROYALTIES

Associations have a wide range of relationships with businesses that want to sell to their members. In some cases, the association may just lend the use of its name to support the sales effort and receive nontaxable royalties in return. If, however, the association does anything more to support the sales effort, care must be used to differentiate between the royalty arrangement and the provision of administrative services that might be taxable. Consult an attorney when entering into such partnerships.

MAILING LIST RENTAL

Association mailing lists provide suppliers with access to a targeted market for their products and services. Some associations have a policy against releasing members' names and addresses to an outside organization. Others rent their lists only to purveyors of certain categories of goods and services. Still others provide members with the option of deleting their names from any mailing list rented to suppliers. The rationale behind such limitations is to decrease the amount of mail received by members and to protect their privacy.

However, because many members genuinely appreciate the opportunity to be notified of new products, services, and special offers, most associations continue to offer their members' names and addresses to suppliers—albeit with certain restrictions.

The most common restriction is that the list is rented—not sold—for one-time use. This guards against suppliers copying the names and addresses and using them for free to do subsequent mailings. Most associations emphasize that member turnover and address changes make lists outdated quickly. They also "salt" the list with addresses of staffers or other people who would report multiple mailings or other apparent infractions of the rental agreement. Another option is for the association to handle the mailing itself and bill the vendor accordingly, so the mailing list is never released outside the organization.

FOUNDATION CONTRIBUTIONS

Suppliers frequently find themselves welcomed on the governance body of foundations whose affiliated or parent associations might not allow them to serve on the board of directors. There are at least two reasons for this. First, suppliers on a foundation's board can more effectively solicit their own colleagues in the vendor community for contributions. Second, foundations provide an opportunity for suppliers interested in the future of the trade or profession to get involved, without having a hand in public policy activities that could create conflict between suppliers and core members.

Foundations seeking contributions from suppliers won't necessarily encounter competition from their parent associations, which may be tapping the same companies for advertising or trade shows. Many large corporations have their own foundations that can contribute to the association foundation without involving the advertising or promotion budgets.

Cautions and Concerns

Tapped to support trade shows, purchase advertising, and invest in other activities, suppliers may seem too good to be true for a cash-strapped association. The

TAXING QUESTIONS

A tax-exempt organization pays unrelated business income tax (UBIT) on its gross income that is all of the following:

- Derived from a trade or business. This refers to any activity designed to produce income from either selling goods or performing services.

- Regularly carried on. Whether seasonal, periodic, or ongoing, this phrase refers to an activity that has the same frequency as it would if conducted by a nonexempt organization.

- Not substantially related to its tax-exempt purpose. The IRS tends to take a case-by-case approach to defining "substantially related." For example, publishing a book would probably be considered as furthering an association's educational purpose and therefore might be nontaxable. Selling coffee mugs with the association's logo would be taxable—even if the proceeds funded a scholarship program.

Given the various IRS regulations—and court challenges to them—it's best to consult an attorney for up-to-date UBIT information.

Internal Revenue Service seems to agree and takes a special interest in the relationship between associations and suppliers. In fact, the IRS popularized the term "associate member" because it needed a label for this special type of member.

The main interest of the IRS stems from the question of whether dues from associate members should be treated as related or unrelated business income. In several recent cases involving 501(c)(5) organizations (agricultural and horticultural organizations and labor unions), the IRS has taken the position that associate members joined primarily to gain access to a community of buyers or to qualify for discounted insurance programs (the formal guidelines were published on March 23, 1995). Because advertising and insurance programs are unrelated business activities for associations, the dues paid specifically to gain access to those services are considered by the IRS to be unrelated business income. With the law in this area still evolving, associations should consult an attorney for guidance on specific applications.

One aspect examined in the cases mentioned above was the involvement of associate members in various activities of the association, particularly their role in governance. In associations where suppliers provide a substantial portion of the revenue stream, supplier members tend to be sought out and integrated into the organizational structure. For example, many organizations reserve one or two seats on their board specifically for associate members. As the IRS sees it, having voting privileges and serving in leadership roles indicate that suppliers are more like "real" members and, therefore, their dues aren't likely to be taxed.

Overall, one out of three associations allows associate members to serve on its board of directors; that number drops to one out of four in individual membership organizations. In three out of five associations (60 percent), however, associate members do not have voting rights. Increasingly, suppliers are asking for a voice in governance. As suppliers provide more revenues for an association through advertising purchases and exhibit space rentals, some want to become more intimately involved with their "investment."

Too, suppliers can benefit from the contacts they make as board members, and they recognize that their future financial health is inextricably linked to the continued health of the business or profession they serve. To the extent that organizational interests and supplier interests dovetail, associations have a strong incentive to create special membership categories and service opportunities for suppliers, perhaps even giving them a voice in governance.

At some point, however, the interests of core members and suppliers are likely to diverge and create controversy. Managing conflicting interests can tax an association executive's diplomatic skills. When suppliers have been fully integrated into the membership and the decision-making process, leaders may fail to vigorously pursue the best interests of the core members for fear of alienating associate members and losing important financial contributions. That, in turn, may alienate primary members.

Therefore, as a matter of policy, it ought to be made clear that when and if the interests of the core members and the supplier community diverge, the association will side with the core members and pursue their interests with all available resources. Doing anything less risks burning down the coop that houses the golden goose. ■

13

Government Relations

Key Points

- Representation on public policy issues is the primary motive for joining a trade association.

- The government relations function encompasses collecting and disseminating information on issues, establishing the organization's stance on the issues, and undertaking advocacy activities aimed at government decision makers.

- Political action committees enable individuals to pool their small contributions to make a bigger impression on a candidate.

Every trade or profession has policy interests it would like to advance, preserve, or protect. Not surprisingly, most associations would identify representing the interests of their members to government as a key benefit of belonging. Indeed, a 1981 study by the Stanford Research Institute pointed out that legislative representation on public policy issues is the primary motive for joining a trade association.

According to *Policies & Procedures in Association Management,* two out of three associations monitor legislation at both the federal and state levels, and a similar percentage (69 percent) have the ability to launch grassroots political activities among members. One-third of associations devote a full-time staff, with an average of three employees, to government relations activities, and 60 percent engage in direct lobbying of regulatory or executive agencies or elected officials.

Because of such statistics, membership organizations in general—and trade associations in particular—are frequently and cynically referred to as "special interests." Yet any collective effort to influence government is not only done on behalf of "special interests" but also sanctioned by the Founding Fathers. The First Amendment to the U.S. Constitution protects the right to peaceably assemble and to petition the government for redress of grievances—a classic definition of government relations by special interests.

A common misconception among the general public is that associations subvert the democratic process by "buying" favorable laws. Although there are no statutory limits on the amount of money that 501(c)(6) organizations may spend on lobbying, actual expenditures related to government relations total far less than those in other areas. The ASAE *Operating Ratio Report,* for example, notes that 501(c)(6) organizations on average spend 5 percent of their total income on government affairs—compared with 12.1 percent on meetings and expositions. Plus, through direct or indirect membership in professional societies, religious associations, employer groups, labor unions, consumer groups, hobby or affinity organizations, and so forth, almost all Americans are represented within the democratic process.

TAKING THE TEST

The rules regulating lobbying by charities differ from those that apply to 501(c)(6) organizations. "Insubstantiality of expenditure" is the watchword for 501(c)(3) associations that engage in government relations.

Unfortunately, the definition of "insubstantial" isn't clear because the IRS addresses it on a case-by-case basis. This uncertainty regarding how to construe "insubstantiality of expenditure" leads some 501(c)(3)s to opt for a "safe harbor" under Section 501(h) of the Internal Revenue Code. That section defines insubstantiality as less than 20 percent of the first $500,000 of the association budget, 15 percent of the second $500,000, 10 percent of the third $500,000, and 5 percent of each subsequent $500,000.

Regardless of its budget, a (c)(3) may not spend more than $1 million on lobbying, which has been narrowly construed under this section of the tax code. (Note, however, that other sections use different definitions of lobbying.) Thus, a (c)(3) association with a $5 million gross budget could, under Section 501(h), spend $400,000 on lobbying and still pass the insubstantiality test.

In recent years, 501(c)(6) associations have had to keep track of expenditures for lobbying under a very broad definition of the term. They must either notify their members of the percent of the dues allocated to lobbying (which then become nondeductible to the member) or pay an *in lieu* tax.

Three Main Thrusts

The government relations function has three distinct parts.

1. Collecting and disseminating information about emerging issues. Associations use a wide variety of techniques to track what various branches of government and other interest groups are doing or considering. One widely used process known as "issues management" typically follows these steps:

- Forecasting the public policy issues that may evolve and predicting their potential effect on members.
- Developing strategies for intervening or participating in those issues.
- Putting the plan into action should the need arise.

Forecasting, although one of the most intriguing aspects of issues management, is frequently ignored by organizations too busy with today's issues to worry about tomorrow's. Unfortunately, the opportunity to exert maximum influence occurs when an issue is beginning to emerge, not when it has nearly run its course. Associations don't serve their members well if they ignore potential issues that, if attended to early enough, might never reach the level of full-fledged crises (see Chapter 14 for more information on issues management).

Associations have some advantages over for-profit businesses when it comes to forecasting. First, by virtue of their lobbying efforts, most already have extensive contacts with decision makers—contacts that can be mined for information about anticipated public policy developments. In addition, given some training and the proper forum, an association's committee members can channel their varying viewpoints and expertise into a valuable forecasting session. Whatever the method used, an association's leaders should set aside time each year to look away from the press of today's business and anticipate future trends.

Issues management also makes good sense from a marketing standpoint. As the association collects intelligence to forecast the future and communicates its findings, it can alert members to changes in the environment and reinforce the necessity for continued commitment to the organization that represents their interests. This public policy "early warning system" greatly helps lobbying efforts—members who are forewarned can be more easily mobilized to contact their legislators or representatives.

2. Agreeing on the organization's stance on the issues through the work of committees and other governance structures. The majority of associations rely on the chief staff executive (72 percent) or the government affairs committee of volunteers (60 percent) to make recommendations on policies related to government affairs. In general, the board of directors makes the final decision on the association's goals in this area.

3. Undertaking advocacy activities to persuade government decision makers to adopt the association's viewpoint. The most familiar advocacy activity, undertaken by six out of ten associations, is using professional, registered lobbyists to carry a message to lawmakers and their staffs.

Although some associations—about one out of three—count on a political action committee and its contributions to get their lobbyists in the door, mobilizing many voters to contact their elected legislators can be more effective. Many organizations concentrate on such a grassroots approach and spend considerable resources to identify and educate "key contacts"—individual members who agree to personally encourage their elected representatives to take a position consistent with the association's objectives.

Key contact programs take advantage of the widespread membership base of associations. Most national individual membership organizations and many corporate-based organizations have at least one member in every congressional or state district. For years, the California Dental Association (CDA), in Sacramento, has attempted to identify the local dentist of each state legislator. As a former CDA executive explains it (with tongue firmly in cheek), the association figures that legislators are especially open to persuasion on dental issues when their own dentist is standing over them, wielding sharp instruments.

Thanks to Web sites, Internet listservers, and broadcast fax technology, associations can communicate almost instantaneously with members and mobilize them for action. In fact, some argue that the explosive growth of the Internet will ultimately encourage a broader and more direct citizen participation in the democratic process. Others say that earlier technologies, such as phone and fax, could well have had the same effect, yet Americans remain lax about voicing their concerns to their elected representatives.

The media provide another opportunity to draw legislators' attention to an association's concerns. This type of advocacy usually involves public policy advertisements in the media most often used by decision makers. Foremost among these would be television network affiliates in Washington, D.C., as well as *the Washington Post*. In addition, less well-known publications—including *The National Journal*, *Roll Call*, and *The Hill*—are also well-read by Washington insiders. Associations also target specific legislators by advertising in hometown papers.

A more active approach to advocacy involves an annual "Day in Washington" or legislative forum. Typically, such an event brings members to Washington or the state capital to be updated on significant public policy positions, trained in how to be effective during the visit, and then turned loose to visit their elected representatives. For a more formal variation on this theme, associations arrange for their members to provide direct testimony to congressional committees with jurisdiction over issues of concern.

Strength in Numbers

When facing a large-scale issue or one that affects diverse populations, associations may team up to form a coalition. Their goal is to unite their voices and make their interests known over the din of many other groups clamoring for attention.

A coalition may bring together seemingly unlikely groups. In the mid-1980s, for example, a coalition of former rivals on many healthcare issues (business, labor, and hospitals) formed to support a new method of paying for hospital care known as Diagnostic Related Groups. The hospitals, which had traditionally aligned with physicians, shifted the balance and the legislation sailed through Congress. As another example, the Society of Nuclear Medicine joined with the Sierra Club to support legislation favoring interstate agreements regarding the disposal of low-level nuclear waste.

Informal coalitions may develop and then evaporate as issues come and go, while others—such as the American Recreation Coalition, of Washington, D.C.—have stood the test of time. Whether long-term or short-lived, coalitions provide a useful mechanism for information exchange, vote counting, and allocation of assignments in pursuit of public policy goals. They typically include lobbyists, individual corporations, and other entities in addition to one or more associations.

Branching Out

An association's government affairs activities will vary depending on where the crucial public policy decisions are made and which branch of government is involved.

- The legislative branch first articulates and then adopts the laws of the country, making Congress the natural focal point for a national organization's lobbying activities. How Congress really works is a lifetime study that transcends any simple chart showing how a bill becomes law. New lobbyists should seek expert advice as they begin to influence the outcomes of congressional action.

- The executive branch, including the White House and myriad departments and regulatory agencies of the federal government, interprets the laws passed by Congress. These interpretations result in administrative agencies propagating literally thousands of new rules and regulations each year.

- The judicial branch upholds or reverses laws that are challenged. Associations may instigate litigation directly or submit *amicus curiae* (friend of the court) briefs to voice their concerns on significant cases.

The federal structure of tripartite government is replicated at the state level and, to some extent, at the county and city levels. Depending on an organization's interests and the location of its members, state or local action may have an equivalent or greater effect than action at the federal level. County medical societies, for example, may be more immediately concerned with the activities of the county public health department than with the federal Department of Health and Human Services. Likewise, local boards of REALTORS® expend much of their government affairs energies on hometown decisions about development and zoning.

Even interest groups outside the realm of business associations have significant agendas vis-a-vis the government. For instance, many 501(c)(4) civic organizations and 501(c)(3) charities have a stake in certain issues, such as unrelated business income tax, nonprofit postal rates, and substantiation of volunteer expenses.

Political Action Committees

"Money is the mother's milk of politics," a quote ascribed to Jesse Unruh, the long-time speaker of California's state assembly, is true to some extent. Given the costs of modern-day campaigns, politicians spend a significant portion of their time ensuring they'll have enough money to run for office again.

Current laws stipulate that only individuals, not corporations, can contribute to campaigns for a federal office. Some states set the same limitation, but others allow corporate contributions to local campaigns. In most cases, public disclosure of contributions over a certain amount is required. For federal campaign contributions, the identification must include the donor's employer.

Political action committees (PACs) are simply one mechanism that enables individuals to pool their small contributions and make a bigger impression on a candidate. Labor unions were the first organizations to formally pool money for use as political contributions. Business and corporate PACs soon followed, all based on the idea that individuals ought to be able to support candidates for whatever reason, whether economic, personal, or emotional. PACs are tightly regulated as to the amount they can contribute and how contributions must be reported. With campaign-finance regulations frequently under review, association executives should remain alert for possible changes.

PAC activity is by no means universal. *Policies & Procedures in Association Management* reports that only one out of three (32 percent) of associations operates a PAC, with trade associations and state/regional organizations the most likely to have one. PAC resources can be used for political education of members, thereby providing a sense of participation in the political process. Because only non-corporate donations can be used for candidate support in a federal campaign, associations can fund the administrative expenses of the PAC from the association's general budget, allowing 100 percent of the contributions to flow directly to their candidates of choice.

The decision to form a PAC should not be taken lightly. The existence of a PAC may raise many politicians' expectations of support, including attendance at fund-raising functions and contributions in excess of the resources likely to be collected. Any association considering a PAC should think about whether it will be able to raise enough money to meet these expectations.

Status Quo or Better Laws?

Some government relations experts observe that associations and other special interests multiply in stable societies and tend, over time, to become resistant to change and protective of their current privileges. Others have persuasively argued that the interplay of ideas put forward by the many disparate interest groups in society enriches and enlivens the debate among decision makers and leads to better public policies. The outcome of this debate remains to be seen, but it certainly merits the attention of association managers.

APPRECIATION FOR THE GRASSROOTS

Museums have opened the eyes of Americans to international wonders from King Tut's tomb to the Soyuz space capsule, and no schoolchild's education is complete without regular field trips to local museums. In 1986, however, federal legislation threatened to put an end to contributions that museums depend on for survival.

Specifically, the 1986 Tax Reform Act limited the tax deductibility of "appreciated property" given to museums and other charities. This meant that donors could deduct gifts of collectibles, securities, and real estate at their original value rather than current market value, which was likely to be much higher. With more than 80 percent of the items in their collections made possible by donations, museums became understandably alarmed.

Undoing the onerous law looked impossible. According to the Joint Committee on Taxation, repeal would cost the U.S. Treasury $417 million in lost taxes over five years. Plus, the media repeatedly played up the angle of removing tax loopholes for wealthy Americans. Standing against this solid wall of resistance was the American Association of Museums (AAM), based in Washington, D.C., with its 2,900 institutional members, 9,000 individual members, and three lobbyists.

In fighting back, AAM first conducted statistical studies of member institutions; those showed a 60 percent drop in donations between 1985 and 1987. AAM also took the initiative to propose specific offsets in the federal budget that would raise $52 million more than the current bill's provisions. Another important step was convincing the media that the real issue was not punishing the rich but preserving vital public institutions.

To get out its messages and broaden its lobbying base, AAM formed the Museum Advocacy Team (MAT) to offer education and training to members and nonmembers alike. MAT participants received an action kit containing the names of their elected officials, instructions for contacting them, and an in-depth explanation of the issues. Rather than providing these voluntary advocates with canned scripts, AAM encouraged them to make the case against the legislation in their own words—a strategy that boosted the quality of contacts with officials.

Computerized databases allowed AAM to pinpoint the most effective advocate for any given issue and elected representative, and fax broadcasts provided almost instantaneous communication with volunteers. These enabled AAM to be more personal and flexible in its grassroots lobbying. At one point, for instance, a Ways and Means Committee member expressed doubts about the offset provisions that AAM had recommended. Within an hour, he received a personal message from the director of a major museum in his district assuring him that the offsets had been well researched and deserved his support. "Dear Ben," the letter began, and it was signed "With love to Myrna."

The battle lasted from 1986 until the Omnibus Budget Reconciliation Act of 1993. But the seven-year effort paid off. By broadening its base, mobilizing its membership, doing its homework, redefining the issue, and presenting positive alternatives, AAM not only secured permanent repeal of the original law but also made the repeal retroactive to 1986—a piece of work that deserves a place in the museum of government relations. ∎

The Public

Key Points

- Effective public relations requires identifying an organization's various publics and tailoring messages to the unique needs of each.

- Key audiences typically include association leaders, members, customers or clients of the association's members, government decision makers and regulators, the media, and the general public.

- The issues management process involves determining what issues are most likely to cause controversy and planning a response.

The world has changed quite a bit since railroad czar Cornelius Vanderbilt uttered his famous four-word philosophy of public relations: "The public be damned." In the intervening century, corporate America has come to realize that, far from being damned, the public must be courted, researched, and communicated with. Otherwise, a business will find it difficult to reach its full potential and ride out the inevitable storms of controversy.

As nonprofit business entities, associations have learned the same lesson. As defined by their resources, almost all associations are very small businesses; about 16 percent of associations have incomes that exceed $10 million, while a medium-size business is usually defined by annual revenues of $50 million or more.

Still, many associations have jumped into public relations (PR) activities with gusto, undertaking ambitious projects on limited budgets and staffs. Fewer than one in three associations (30 percent) have a PR department, and the majority of those departments also handle other responsibilities ranging from government affairs to magazine publishing.

The person in charge of PR typically faces the challenge of leveraging small expenditures into a highly influential campaign. To succeed, two elements are necessary. First, the association must do the right things, from conducting valuable research to mounting a major trade show, that fall into the category of PR "programming." The slickest, most sophisticated communications campaign in the world can't create goodwill for a do-nothing organization. As one PR practitioner once said, the key to good public relations is to do things right and then talk about them.

Second, PR campaigns must be targeted carefully. Given the number of messages cluttering the media and the price paid for those messages, reaching the general public is virtually impossible for small businesses, such as associations. Fortunately, good PR is more tightly focused than mass-market advertising.

The very term "public relations" is probably a misnomer because experts agree that a huge, monolithic public doesn't exist. Rather, "the public" comprises many distinct publics, each with different opinions and information needs.

Consequently, PR requires identifying an organization's various publics and tailoring messages to the unique needs of each.

Key Audiences

Specific publics vary from one association to another. It can be helpful to identify key audiences as targets. Each target represents a specific public that you want to reach with a message: association leaders, current members, potential members, suppliers, customers or clients of members, related organizations and their members, government decision makers and regulators, the media, and the general public.

A target might be subdivided. For instance, within the "media" target audience, the trade press and the public general media will have different needs and require different strategies.

Targets might overlap. For instance, the association's leadership target will be totally enclosed by the membership target like a bull's eye. In some instances, some suppliers will be both suppliers and members and will be visualized by overlapping circles. Each association should draw its own schematic of target audiences.

The target model visually clarifies the pattern and interdependence of an association's various publics. Of course, identifying publics goes beyond a simple exercise in conceptualization. To some extent, the target audience for the PR campaign will automatically dictate the strategies, techniques, and media employed. Key publics and goals include members, members' customers, government regulators and legislators, the general public, and the media.

MEMBERS

Keeping members happy and well-informed should be a primary goal of any association's PR efforts—it's analogous to customer relations in the for-profit business realm. Constantly reminding members of all the association does on their behalf should be relatively easy given the existing communications vehicles (print and e-mail newsletters, journals, and magazines) members already receive.

But effective public relations goes beyond selling members on the virtues of the association. Members also need an easy, convenient way to air their gripes and submit their suggestions. Studies conducted by the retail industry have found that, for every customer who takes the time to complain, 12 others withdraw their business without saying a word. In addition, one unsatisfied customer typically tells 10 to 16 other people of his or her unhappy experience.

Assuming that these statistics hold true in the association field, it becomes an economic imperative to provide members a means of filing complaints and receiving satisfactory answers to their concerns. The easier this process is, the greater the likelihood that they won't quietly withdraw their membership. For this reason, some organizations actively solicit comments and complaints through postage-paid reply cards; e-mail, fax, or Web-based customer satisfaction surveys; or toll-free telephone numbers.

MEMBERS' CUSTOMERS

Improving an industry's or profession's image among its customers is accomplished primarily through education. Customer satisfaction, after all, is generally not a function of any objective standard but rather of customer expectations. By educating customers, associations help to shape expectations and bring them in line with reality, thus improving customer satisfaction.

The International Fabricare Institute, based in Silver Spring, Maryland, does this through educational brochures that help customers understand what happens when their clothes are cleaned. One brochure aimed at male customers reveals that expensive, name-brand suits often conceal an inexpensive lining that shrivels and puckers when the suit is cleaned. It goes on to tell dissatisfied customers how to contact the garment's maker—rather than the dry cleaner—when such a situation occurs.

Many associations help market their members' goods and services to communities of buyers, often relying on special assessment funds to fund the programs. The Pork Producers Council ("The Other White Meat") and the Dairy Council, Inc. ("Got Milk?") both advertise and market their members' products directly to consumers; the latter spends millions annually. Other organizations operate trade shows for the public, such as associations of automobile dealers sponsoring car shows.

In the professional arena, medical societies and bar associations often operate referral services to connect potential clients with members in the same area. Although valuable and popular, such services require great care when it comes to liability issues and fairness in the allocation of referrals.

GOVERNMENT REGULATORS AND LEGISLATORS

Although small, this public can have a significant influence on an industry or profession. Fortunately, the government's size enables associations to easily target decision makers. Everyone on Capitol Hill, for instance, reads *Roll Call* or *The Hill* (or both), while regulators in executive branch agencies can't start their day without *The Washington Post*. This explains why so many association ads appear in the Washington media as well as in newspapers of various state capitals.

The independent studies released by think tanks and universities offer another effective tool for reaching government decision makers. Such third-party endorsements of an association's position can prove invaluable in the passage of friendly legislation. In 1995, for instance, a conservative North Carolina think tank attacked the federally funded Center for Substance Abuse Prevention (CSAP), saying that, "In short, taxpayers have paid to arm neo-prohibitionists for political battle" at a cost of some $239 million annually.

CSAP had long been the bane of the National Beer Wholesalers Association (NBWA), of Alexandria, Virginia, which believed the agency wanted to eradicate even "responsible drinking." NBWA bought hundreds of copies of the think tank's report and flooded Capitol Hill with an ostensibly objective, third-party endorsement of its own position. Soon after, the House severely cut CSAP's budget appropriation, virtually killing off the agency.

GENERAL PUBLIC

In spite of the high expense and difficulty in measuring results, many industries and professions launch campaigns aimed at building goodwill with the general public. This type of PR becomes especially important when an industry has been under direct attack or clouded by suspicion. Thus, in the early 1990s, when federal healthcare reform proposals threatened their livelihood, the medical profession, health insurance companies, and health management organizations regularly purchased full-page "image ads" in national publications.

Attempts to influence the attitudes of the general public usually don't work unless the association can successfully mobilize a wide range of activities on the local level. Such efforts might include organizing members to give speeches before local civic groups or encouraging local chapters to undertake high-profile charitable activities that will attract favorable media coverage.

Another way to leverage scarce public relations resources is to focus national efforts on opinion leaders rather than the masses. Once an association has won over the opinion leaders, it hopes that a favorable impression will trickle down to others within their sphere of influence. That's why image advertising generally appears in newspapers rather than on radio or TV. Newspapers not only require greater effort on the part of the user but also provide more in-depth coverage than the broadcast media. For these reasons, newspaper readership is skewed upward in terms of education and income—the kind of people likely to be opinion leaders.

THE MEDIA

Public relations is, by no means, just advertising. Newsworthy acts need to be brought to the attention of the media. But remember, however, the media—not associations—determine newsworthiness. The association leader's task is to understand the media decision makers' needs well enough to structure the association's story in a way that will appeal to the media's market.

Public Relations in a Crisis

The occasional crisis—an unexpected, uncontrollable event that places the association or its members in a bad light—may hit even those associations with exemplary PR efforts. Or something could occur that gives the association an opportunity to show itself in a positive light. Although it's impossible to anticipate every situation that could precipitate a crisis, analysis and planning can help the association avoid being caught with nothing to say. This process, known as issues management, depends on staff members and volunteer leaders looking into the future to determine which issues are most likely to cause controversy.

BURNING ISSUES

Few would deny that the tobacco industry in America is fighting an uphill public relations battle. Government regulators consider adding more than printed warnings on cigarette packs. Health-conscious Americans, encouraged by media reports on the dangers of smoking, use everything from nicotine patches to hypnotism to kick the habit. And individual smokers who continue to light up often find themselves under attack from nonsmokers.

Suppose, in this hostile environment, that the fictional Cigarette Manufacturers Association (CMA) creates a print advertising campaign to bolster the beleaguered image of the smoking public (Audience: customers of members). Accordingly, it earmarks money to create print ads featuring close-up portraits and quotations of popular Hollywood stars who are smokers.

The ads thrill the targeted public, who believe they have someone speaking out for them and guarding their rights. But other CMA publics aren't so thrilled, especially the chair of the Food and Drug Administration (Audience: government regulators), who sees a popular actress luring teenage girls to start smoking because cigarettes will make them glamorous and sexy. He starts calling allies on Capitol Hill, urging them to pass a bill that bars the tobacco industry from all print advertising.

Other publics are affected as well. When CMA lobbyists (Audience: employees) hit the halls of Congress the next day, angry senators demand an explanation of the ads. *The Washington Post* (Audience: media) gets wind of the controversy and makes it a front-page story. Hundreds of angry readers (Audience: general public) deluge magazines with letters to the editor, and many cancel their subscriptions. One magazine's publisher calls his golfing buddy, the chair of CMA's board of governors, and demands that the association publicly apologize for any misunderstandings created by the ad.

The chair assures his friend that the ad campaign was created without his approval and hastily arranges an emergency conference call with other board members (Audience: volunteer governance). Angry at being left out of the loop, a number of them call for the resignation of the executive director, who approved the ads.

Result: An ad campaign targeted at a single public has affected nearly every other public of CMA and caused untold damage.

In the medical profession, for instance, some likely crisis scenarios might include a government reform of healthcare, a highly publicized series of wrongful death cases, a viral epidemic, or allegations of financial mismanagement on the part of the association. Typically, after brainstorming possible crises, the participants apply a series of questions to each scenario:

1. On a scale of improbable to inevitable, what is the likelihood that this crisis will become a reality?

2. If it seems likely, what is the time frame—six months? One year? Five years?

3. On a scale of absolutely nothing to complete damage control, how much can the association hope to accomplish should the crisis become a reality?

4. If damage control seems possible, what would it cost? Does the association have the resources available?

5. What would be the cost of completely ignoring the issue?

The list of possible crises could go on and on, but most experts agree that 10 is the maximum number of issues that can be managed effectively. This means that after the brainstorming session has concluded, the association must trim its list to a manageable number of issues.

Then the real work begins. For each crisis scenario, the association must formulate a response. The response will vary from one situation to another, but at a minimum it should include a mechanism for rapidly notifying key officials and designating a primary spokesperson who will ensure the organization communicates a unified, coherent message. Finally, the association should develop a series of talking points for the designated spokesperson to review and rehearse. When 60 Minutes calls at 7 a.m. to ask about a breaking scandal, it's reassuring to know that the questions have been anticipated and some thoughtful answers are as close as the filing cabinet.

A rapid-response plan requires cooperation and trust between staff and leaders. Board members should participate in the issues management process or, at the very least, approve the response plans for each crisis scenario. The chief elected officer may also serve as the designated spokesperson; this is especially common in individual membership organizations, while nearly two-thirds of trade associations select the chief staff executive as the primary spokesperson. (Rarely, in less than 5 percent of associations, does a PR staff person fill that role.)

Whoever is selected, the spokesperson must be prepared to speak authoritatively from the moment the crisis occurs. The media often interpret "no comment" as stonewalling or an attempt to cover up guilt. As leadership changes, the association should review and update its plans—otherwise, it may find itself in the embarrassing position of having a new CEO publicly contradicting the organization's official position.

The issues management process may seem like a lot of work for a plan that may never be used. After all, three out of four associations responding to *Policies & Procedures in Association Management* hadn't experienced a disaster or media crisis in the preceding three years. Still, a bit of flame-proofing now may well avoid major flare-ups in the future. Plus, responding coolly and competently when faced with a crisis makes management look exceeding capable—and looking good is what public relations is all about.

Of course, it's possible that a crisis will develop for which no one anticipated or planned. So, in addition to an issues management program, associations should have a generic crisis plan at the ready. At a minimum, it should describe who will be involved in the response, how they can be reached on short notice, and who will act as the immediate spokesperson. ■

Foundations and Fund Raising

Key Points

- The primary functions of association foundations include education, scholarship programs, and research.

- Establishing a foundation presents opportunities to involve people outside the core membership—particularly members of the supplier community—in leadership roles.

- Tax-deductible contributions can be solicited via direct mail, voluntary assessments, special events, and major gift requests.

Associations find themselves caught between business and charity. The successful association must operate like the former, but many of its activities are more akin to the latter. Indeed, many associations share the same tax-exempt status, 501(c)(3), as traditional charities, such as churches and not-for-profit health and education organizations.

Approximately 39 percent of associations have created separate charitable foundations. These sister organizations provide not only an outlet for an association's charitable activities but also, in many cases, a powerful fund-raising machine. For just as dues are the lifeblood of 501(c)(6) associations, tax-deductible donations keep 501(c)(3) charities alive.

Some organizations have opted for an "If we build it, they will come" approach; in other words, simply forming a foundation would ensure that donations came pouring in. Although any foundation will undoubtedly focus on fund raising, "collecting money" is hardly a sufficient purpose to list in the articles of incorporation. The association must decide on a deeper, more fundamental purpose for its new organization.

According to *Policies & Procedures in Association Management*, the primary functions of association foundations include education (undertaken by 73 percent), scholarship programs (46 percent), and research (37 percent). Some foundations, for instance, offer grants to encourage innovation in the industry or profession or operate as a think tank to research the future of the field. The foundation should codify its raison d'etre in its statement of purpose.

Operational Issues

Before establishing a 501(c)(3) foundation, the association must carefully consider governance issues, especially the extent to which the parent organization maintains control. One solution is to create overlapping boards. If board members are already overworked, however, burdening them with an additional responsibility makes it likely that the new entity will not get off the ground. In addition, such an arrangement could attract the attention of the IRS.

On the other hand, a completely different board may move the foundation in directions different from or even in conflict with those of the parent organization. It's not unusual for a spin-off organization to develop a life of its own and enter into activities that compete with those of the association. This dilemma is often solved by expanding the board of the parent association to reduce the workload of individual members, then asking several members to also serve on the board of the foundation, along with new members.

The establishment of a foundation presents opportunities to involve people outside the core membership—particularly members of the supplier community— in leadership roles. Giving suppliers a high-prestige position on the board, for example, often carries the expectation of active participation in the foundation's fund-raising activities.

As for financial relationships, slightly less than 20 percent of foundations pay a management fee to their parent organizations. More commonly (31 percent), the foundation pays the association for services rendered on an as-needed basis. One in four foundations (26 percent) shares overhead with the association.

The termination provisions for foundations require that remaining assets go to another 501(c)(3) organization, not to the association.

Finding the Funds

Whatever its purpose, a foundation inevitably expends much time and effort on fund raising. Indeed, members of a foundation board should expect to participate in fund raising; or, as some in the field have commented, "Board members should give, get, or get off."

Fund raising, whether related to an annual fund, special project, or capital campaign, can take a wide variety of forms:

- Voluntary assessments. Small, grassroots donations can add up to a considerable portion of a foundation's overall budget. In some cases, the parent association includes on the annual dues invoice a line for a specific "voluntary contribution" to the foundation. Members who don't wish to make the donation simply deduct the amount from their dues—but relatively few do so.

- Direct mail. This approach—the most prevalent means of soliciting grassroots donations—is most likely to succeed when the mail piece is targeted to specific prospects and their interests. For instance, a campaign to raise money for research into retailing techniques should point out explicitly how donors' businesses will benefit from the study's results.

- Special events. These often include recognition banquets, silent and live auctions, and a wide variety of -thons (phone-a-thons, bike-a-thons, dance-a-thons, and so forth). While such events generate both excitement and donations, the fund-raising literature suggests that the dollar return is relatively low in relation to the number of hours required to mount them.

A FIRM FOUNDATION

Historically, the Foundation of the American Society of Association Executives, Washington, D.C., was a jack-of-all-trades organization that relied on annual fund raisers and special events to finance a variety of educational, research, and publishing projects. In 1993, the ASAE Foundation redefined its mission to focus on four areas: leadership development (improving the skills and abilities of volunteers and staff), strategic research (trend analysis, environmental scanning, and public policy research), public outreach (correcting misapprehensions about the association sector and promoting its unique place in American society), and innovation (measurable improvement of management processes).

This ambitious plan required an equally ambitious budget. Rather than continue to fund projects year-by-year, the foundation board created a permanent endowment that would generate interest in perpetuity. Using the foundation's annual budget of $500,000 and allowing for future growth, planners calculated an endowment goal of $5 million.

Reaching this goal first required development of a case statement—a document explaining the reasons and benefits for the foundation's restructuring. An outside consultant was retained to help the foundation's three full-time employees, and the firm conducted a feasibility study that involved presenting the case statement to about 70 people from the various sectors whose support would be vital. Armed with results from the feasibility study (in this case, most potential donors wanted more information on how the foundation would use the interest income from the endowment), the foundation categorized its universe of potential donors and assembled a leadership team for the campaign.

First, the leaders focused on obtaining major gifts from the supplier community, which included the hospitality industry, convention and visitors bureaus, and insurers. The supplier selected to chair the campaign brought with him a leadership gift of $300,000. Working with him was a Campaign Executive Committee composed of representatives of each market segment. In turn, each representative helped recruit additional volunteers to make contact with suppliers, associations, and association executives.

The quiet phase of the campaign—before any public announcement of the goal—lasted just four months and generated about $2.6 million in contributions. The public, grassroots phase began in March 1994 and involved tens of thousands of contacts via letters, phone calls, and personal visits. Just five months later, thanks to the work of staff and hundreds of volunteers, the ASAE Foundation had raised $6 million—20 percent over goal. Grassroots contributions represented $1 million, with a similar amount coming from convention and visitors bureaus. The balance of $4 million flowed in from associate members—which certainly illustrates the importance of maintaining good relations with the supplier community.

■ Major gifts. As important as $25 and $50 donations may be, there's nothing like a large gift of $5,000 or $10,000 to give a foundation the financial boost it needs to undertake a major project. Attracting major gifts, however, requires an entirely different strategy than grassroots appeals. Large-scale campaigns require significant planning, including prospect research to identify the interests of potential donors, one-on-one solicitations, appropriate techniques for publicly recognizing large gifts, and a range of options for giving (such as living trusts and estate planning). Many foundations retain outside consultants to assist with the solicitation of major gifts.

Not surprisingly, association foundations, like other charities, are subject to a range of rules and regulations. For example, varying rules and regulations in the 50 states set differing fees and reporting requirements for conducting fundraising activities. In addition, the foundation's tax status and the rules for tax deductibility speak only to the United States, so global organizations enjoy limited benefits. All of these issues need to be fully explored before the structure of the foundations is established. ■

Strategic Planning

Key Points

- Strategic planning enables an association to establish a reasonable framework for making short-term tactical decisions in an uncertain environment.

- The planning process can bring a sense of identity and priority back to an association's activities and help leaders achieve consensus.

- The paradox inherent in strategic planning is that an association must work the plan—yet remain flexible and open to change.

*Change—how to anticipate, manage, and survive it—
tops the priority list at virtually every association.* And
it raises numerous questions: How can an association maintain a steady course in
a rapidly changing environment when its elected leadership turns over every year
or two? How can an organization structure itself to be fast, flexible, and effective
in decision making so opportunities aren't lost? What skills must leaders and staff
develop to function effectively in an environment where change is the rule, not the
exception?

Associations constantly strive to balance the need for time-consuming participation in the decision-making process with the growing necessity to react quickly and flexibly to changing conditions. The strategic planning process, first
embraced by businesses and nonprofits in the 1980s, serves as a useful tool for
achieving this balance.

Why Plan Strategically?

Many associations represent industries or professions in a state of flux—take
healthcare associations, for example, or those that represent the telecommunications or computer industries. Strategic planning can help them establish a reasonable framework for making short-term tactical decisions in an uncertain
environment.

But the process also proves valuable in situations where change is less earth-
shattering, where existing plans must simply be modified or updated. Perhaps a
controversy forces an association to focus more resources on government relations or public relations, areas that previously had been taken for granted. As conditions in the external environment change, internal adaptations follow as the
organization tentatively enters into new relationships and programs. If a strategic
plan existed before, the association must adapt it to fit the new reality.

Other benefits of strategic planning include:

- Providing focus. A problem common to many associations is the desire to be all
  things to all categories and subcategories of members. Every idea or project has

its champion, and the organization may be reluctant to say no or to set priorities. As a result, many projects and programs are undertaken without sufficient staffing or financing because resources are simply spread too thin. Strategic planning can bring a sense of identity and priority to the association's activities.

■ Achieving consensus. Even if the strategic planning process doesn't change the organization's goals, the agreement achieved can help both staff and elected leaders implement existing plans more efficiently. It can also reenergize a bored or complacent leadership corps.

Steps in the Process

While a step-by-step process applies in most instances, each organization must decide how to execute those steps to balance participation with time and resources. For instance, the planning process can range from a two-year project requiring multiple meetings of many members to an intensive one- or two-day retreat exclusively for key leaders and staff. While it's desirable for associations to implement a process with broad participation, a short time frame, and low cost, the best they can realistically hope for is two out of the three characteristics.

The most common steps in the strategic planning process are:

1. Assign Roles. A small group of people usually has the task of shepherding the organization through the strategic planning process. Whatever its title or composition—executive committee, association officers, strategic planning committee—this group is intimately involved in developing the framework for the overall process.

Different parts of the organization will play different roles, ranging from providing input and analyzing data in the early phases to deciding on the shape and structure of the plan and its implementation schedule. To fill these roles, associations typically tap various constituencies: past presidents, board members, officers, staff, committee chairs, the membership at large, and, in some cases, nonmembers who can offer a perspective on the marketplace or environment in which the organization operates.

Because members may be unfamiliar with strategic planning or prefer the assistance of someone who has no vested interest in the results, many associations hire outside facilitators to help manage the process. These facilitators may be professional consultants or association executives from other organizations with experience in strategic planning.

2. Review the mission statement. Most organizations already have a mission statement, frequently found in their bylaws. In addition, the articles of incorporation contain a statement of purpose that sets the legal limits of authority for the organization. Although articles of incorporation can be amended, it's important to keep these limits in mind from the outset of the planning process.

Reviewing the mission is a significant part of the strategic planning process. In fact, disagreement over the organization's mission strongly points to the need to go through the process. Sometimes this disagreement is so sharp that members choose to review the current mission as a baseline, recognizing that they may modify it as additional information comes to light during the planning process.

Mission statements should be general rather than specific and usually don't include "how to" components, such as the types of programs, projects, and activities the organization will undertake (that material should appear in the general objectives). Some organizations also develop a vision that sweeps aside political, economic, and other constraints to focus on what the organization could be under ideal circumstances. In contrast, mission statements are based on implicit assumptions about the organization's limited resources and therefore tend to be somewhat modest.

3. Collect data. Before the planning process gets underway, committee members should know everything possible about the needs and nature of members and prospective members. This information generally takes the form of member needs surveys, data on the results of focus groups, demographic studies, existing market data, organizational and financial audits, the articles of incorporation, and a current set of bylaws.

Associations that conduct basic research and assemble information from various areas are more likely to create a plan that is both realistic and helpful. Plans based on data are significantly better than those that simply thread together the varying perceptions of the people who take part in the process. Data, even if not determinative, help people form opinions and give participants a better grasp of the reality facing the association.

4. Scan the environment. An environmental scan is an evaluation of the threats and opportunities presented by the "outside world." This step forces managers to focus on the wider environment rather than day-to-day operational matters and internal politics. It encourages them to look beyond current crises, administrative matters, and the publications typically at hand and pay attention to information coming from other areas that eventually may affect the trade or profession.

One way to divide the world into manageable chunks is to brainstorm the outcomes of social, technological, economic, and political trends, estimating the likelihood and effect of each. The strategic planning committee may want to call on outside experts to identify those trends, methodically search external literature for additional information, and bring a variety of perspectives to the discussion.

Rather than focusing on external trends, some organizations generate a list of assumptions about the future. This is simply another way of seeing the organization and its trade or profession in a larger context. It has the added benefit of allowing readers of the strategic plan to understand the assumptions underlying specific proposals.

5. Assess strengths and weaknesses. Once the committee has identified external threats and opportunities, it focuses on the nature of the organization itself. Nothing but a hard look at reality will do. The group should examine staff competence, the volunteer decision-making process, member participation, benefits, and all other aspects of the organization. To prepare for this step, some associations find it helpful to hire an outside expert to conduct an objective evaluation or management audit.

6. Agree on the mission statement. Although consensus on the mission statement is vital to the first few steps, participants' views may have changed in light of what they have since learned about the external environment and the association's internal workings. They might worry, for instance, that the continuation of certain external trends could render today's mission statement obsolete.

Crafting the mission statement requires answering strategic questions that will shape the future. These questions include:

- Who should our core members be?
- What are their essential needs that we are uniquely positioned to provide?
- What must we do to adapt to major changes in our environment?
- How might our relationships with suppliers change?
- What other methods might be used to deliver products and services?

7. Set general objectives. Once the planning group has reached consensus on the mission statement, it turns to developing general objectives for the organization to focus on in the mid-term future (three to five years). Because programs and policies will flow directly out of these objectives, a group consensus is necessary.

Although they vary significantly from one association to another, goals tend to fall into the following categories: developing new services for members, attracting new members, representing the interests of the trade or profession, improving the image of the trade or profession, improving the quality of goods and services produced by the trade or profession, increasing educational outreaches to members, and increasing research efforts. Measures of performance should be identified and targeted results agreed upon.

At this point, many associations circulate a draft to the membership and ask various committees and other subgroups to identify how the objectives are to be reached.

8. Identify measurable activities. This step involves identifying the specific projects, programs, or activities that will lead to achievement of the general objectives. The key here is measurability. Each project or program should include a clear statement of how much and by when. If appropriate, a measure of member satisfaction or some other indicator of quality should also be identified.

Without measurements, associations find it virtually impossible to assess whether they've made any progress. For instance, if the general objective is increasing membership and the specific program is a direct-mail membership marketing campaign, some numerical targets and deadlines must be included. Otherwise, the association may proclaim victory with the addition of one new member, regardless of how long or how much it took to attract that person or how many others dropped out in the meantime.

Including measurable objectives in the plan often meets with stiff resistance at first. It's one thing to say, "We're going to do better," but quite another to say, "Here's how much and by when." The former allows interpretation and uncertainty; the latter creates expectations that lead to accountability. Accountability becomes especially threatening when there is no baseline against which to measure improvement. The planning committee should clarify that, the first time out, performance will be considered satisfactory when it comes somewhat close to the targeted results. Then the next time quantifiable goals are set, they'll be more accurate.

Clearly, if the cost of measurement exceeds the value of the activity, that measurement is not appropriate and should be excluded.

9. Set priorities. It usually becomes apparent that the association has the resources to carry out about one-quarter of the measurable activities. The solution is at once simple and excruciatingly difficult: determine which activities take precedence over others. A variety of techniques can help a planning group develop a set of priorities. They include:

- Have each participant rate each item on a scale of 1 to 10.
- Give each participant a set number of votes that can be spread among the options or all cast for a single favorite. If the options are listed on paper along the walls, give each voter a set number of colored stick-on labels with which to vote.
- Have participants develop personal lists of priorities and aggregate the data.
- Pair each item with every other item and force each participant to make a choice between the two. The data are then aggregated.

No matter what the technique, the priority-setting exercise will tend to reflect support for those activities most closely tied to the association's mission. Although desirable, this outcome overlooks activities that aren't closely related to the mission but might generate resources. Trade shows and advertising sales in the association's periodicals, for example, aren't directly linked to the mission and may receive a low priority ranking—yet they're important sources of income. Moving these "cash cows" to a higher priority might enable the association to undertake more activities that are strongly related to its mission.

10. Allocate resources. For this step, the planning group starts at the top of the priority list and budgets the financial resources, staff time, and volunteer time needed for each activity. Once one of these resources has been used up, the remaining projects are dropped from the list. If priorities have been established properly, the most important programs will receive time and funding while others are wait-listed pending increased resources.

Each item getting the green light is added to the annual work plan or the existing budget structure. This step, the integration of the budgeting process into the strategic plan, is crucial. An individual is assigned to ensure that it's completed.

A NEW PRESCRIPTION

When President Clinton took office in 1993, his administration lost little time in shining the spotlight of public attention on soaring medical costs. The entire healthcare industry came under suspicion, including the pharmaceutical companies represented by the Pharmaceutical Manufacturers Association (PMA). In addition to the political pressures, PMA's members faced other challenges: industry consolidation, layoffs, and the rising influence of HMOs and insurance companies in doctors' selection of medications.

Given this turmoil, pharmaceutical companies looked to their trade association for help. Unfortunately, PMA's mission statement had been written years earlier: The rambling, 600-word document mentioned virtually every single aspect of the association's work—from helping the World Health Organization improve the health of people in developing countries to maximizing the therapeutic effectiveness of their medicines—but provided little guidance.

PMA's board elected to swallow a bitter pill and open every aspect of the association to scrutiny: its identity, purpose, priorities, governance structure, and even its name. With guidance from an outside consulting firm that conducted a management audit, the staff and the board spent almost a year digging up data, asking questions, brainstorming, developing flow charts, and asking more questions.

When the strategic planning process had concluded, the re-christened Pharmaceutical Research and Manufacturers of America (PhRMA), of Washington, D.C., had a new vision as well as a new name. Once staff and leaders had done the hard work of figuring out what the association should be, a new mission statement came easily. Half as long as the original, the new mission statement focused on policy concerns and the external environment. Moreover, it listed a set of "guiding values" (realistic and objective, cost conscious, results oriented, and so forth) to shape the work of the association.

Elements of Good Planning

Some of the top-priority projects, programs, and activities will stretch over multiple calendar or fiscal years. Unfortunately, too many multi-year plans merely incorporate fixed assumptions about the rates of change in costs—postage will go up an average of 7 percent for the next three years while paper costs will increase 3 percent, and so forth. Although such assumptions are necessary, the real challenge is to assess the effect of changes in what the organization will be doing—not just change the costs of doing the same thing.

Good planning also makes clear that the role of the association's leaders is to execute the plan, even if those leaders weren't in office when the plan was formulated. Of course, should external circumstances change significantly, the leaders must be able to respond. That's why a strategic plan needs to be regularly reviewed and revised to remain viable.

Real strategic changes don't occur often. Still, an association should review its mission and objectives every three to five years, depending on the volatility of the environment in which it and its members operate. The greater the volatility and rate of change, the more frequent the review. Ignoring the fact that it operates in a world of constant change condemns an association to eventual obsolescence.

This paradox—work the plan, yet stay flexible—is often difficult to grasp. To the extent that the environment is stable and its projections reasonably accurate, an association should work the plan. But any strategic plan is based on assumptions that may prove wrong. In fact, the futurist William Renfro argues that, "The most likely future isn't." If the most likely future is 20 percent likely to occur, the eventual reality will probably lie in the other 80 percent.

While planning is better than not planning, associations must recognize and adjust to new and unexpected realities. In other words, plan—but stay alert!

BIG PICTURE VERSUS CLOSE-UP

Is strategic planning an oxymoron? In his book, *The Rise and Fall of Strategic Planning,* Henry Mintzberg argues that it is. At the core of his argument is the assumption that strategy is an intuitive process of synthesis. On the other hand, planning is deconstructive—it breaks things down into their components.

True, strategy relates to major goals, objectives, and an organization's mission. Planning focuses on how to get there—the detailed steps and implementation. If Mintzberg is correct, association leaders should focus their time on the big picture, on aligning the organization with the trends they believe will shape the future. The planning steps—specific projects, programs, and activities—need to be developed by committees and staff, consistent with the mission.

This isn't to say that leaders can ignore practical realities or that the planners can overlook changes in the environment over which no one has control. Instead, the leaders must look to the planners and executors of current programs for clues about how the future is developing. Mintzberg also says that real strategic change frequently takes place at the margins of the organization, where the services are being delivered. That means planners must remain aware of changes in the larger environment as well. ∎

Chapter

17

Trends Forecasting

Key Points

- A key process in strategic planning is the evaluation of social, technological, economic, and political trends that confront the organization and the trade or profession it represents.

- As observers of the outside world, chief staff executives must think outside the normal constraints and read more than the business publications or trade press directly related to the industry or profession.

- More formal methods for identifying trends include analyzing demographic data, convening an expert panel, and formulating what-if scenarios.

Back in the late 1980s, how many would have predicted the fall of the Iron Curtain—or the rapid evolution of the Internet and its profound influence on association activities? In fact, some people argue that we should not bother trying to assess what developments the future may hold. The future, they say, is essentially unknowable—too many wild cards can surprise us and change what, otherwise, are reasonable expectations. In addition, with many items clamoring for attention day to day, there's simply no time for long-term thinking.

These observations are true, to a certain extent. Yet, if association executives are to develop flexibility of mind and take seriously their responsibilities as stewards of organizations, efforts must be made to think carefully and analytically about the future. At the least, thinking about likely futures increases the ability to respond when new developments do emerge.

Strategy, according to one definition, refers to the alignment of an organization's activities with its external environment. A key process in strategic planning is the evaluation of social, technological, economic, and political trends that confront the organization and the trade or profession it represents.

Basic Techniques

An association's chief staff executive not only serves as an advocate for the trade or profession to the outside world but also as an observer of the outside world on behalf of the association. To do that effectively, it's necessary to think outside the normal constraints and to read more than the business publications or trade press directly related to the industry or profession.

Beyond general observation and personal reading, here are more formal ways to identify developing trends.

- *Networking.* Conversations within your community of practice, your association, and with others about what they see coming just over the horizon can stimulate your own insights about what the future may bring. Association executives tend to feel comfortable in an informal networking environment because they meet with one another regularly at events sponsored by allied societies, ASAE, and other groups.

Many association executives also form their own networks of people whom they respect. The conversation in such groups, however, usually revolves around how to solve existing problems. It would also be helpful to include time to discuss what people see coming down the track. What kinds of things are happening in their industry? What's the rate of consolidation in their profession? What economic and political issues are surfacing?

- *Identifying and Observing Precursors.* Things don't happen everywhere at the same time; some states tend to be on the leading edge of legislative and regulatory matters. For instance, many significant modifications broadening liability in tort law first occurred in California; Minnesota was a precursor state for the wide expansion of health maintenance organizations and managed care. Observation of precursor states provides lead time for thinking through a development and looking at successful responses to the changes that are coming.

Look at your trade or profession and identify the states or cities where developments typically surface first. Then, keep tabs on what's happening. All too often, a development occurs in one location and is accepted eventually, while other states and locations remain clueless. Consider the evolution of healthcare: Health maintenance organizations (HMOs) emerged in a number of states and quickly took hold, yet groups in other states denied that the same could happen to them. Ten years after health maintenance organizations and managed care had become widespread in Minnesota and California, a visit to a medical society in Illinois found them just discovering the possibility of managed care and going through the same emotional responses that had occurred elsewhere.

- *Demographic Analysis.* Looking at available data and statistical patterns can be helpful in projecting long-term trends. Certain demographic information, such as the population by age, may point to the need for future programs and services. If your association deals with education, for instance, tracking the birth rate will enable you to anticipate the need for the physical housing of students for many years to come. Or, if you are the American Contract Bridge League (ACBL) and track demographics, you may know that the average age of members is consistently rising. Supplied with that knowledge, ACBL must either adapt to having a significantly smaller membership as existing members die or undertake major activities to encourage the spread of interest in contract bridge.

Other important data to consider tracking include income, geographic distribution, market growth or decline within the industry, dispersion rate of new technologies, and diversity (particularly any changes anticipated in the workforce). For professional organizations, mode of practice needs to be observed regularly. For example, tracking modes of practice enabled organized medicine to prepare for the transition from physicians as independent, solo practitioners to members of group practices. To uncover relevant statistics, look to the U.S. Department of Labor, the U.S. Department of Commerce, or your association's own database.

- *Expert Panel:* "Oh, no," you're probably thinking, "not another committee." Yet properly constructed and used, an expert panel group can provide considerable insight into the future of an industry or profession. By and large, expert panels serve as distant early warning systems for issues. Clearly, the earlier you are aware of an issue, the earlier you can begin preparing to meet its challenges head-on.

MEMBERS AS ORACLES

The Delphi Technique offers one way to harness the capabilities of a large and diverse expert panel. The Rand Corporation developed this technique as a means of forecasting technological developments, after it noted people's reluctance to speak up in groups. The larger the group, Rand observed, the greater the reluctance. Not wanting to be considered foolish or risk being embarrassed in front of the group, most people shy away from articulating strong, and possibly unpopular, positions.

The Delphi Technique uses the following process to build or identify consensus across a large range of individuals on issues that might solicit a wide range of responses.

1. Questions are solicited from an expert panel and then assembled into a logical series. The questions must be phrased in a way that encourages a quantitative response, typically expressed as a percentage. For example: "What is the likelihood that Congress will vote to make trade show revenue unrelated business income by the year 2004?"

2. Each member of the panel is solicited for answers to the questions. They are encouraged to respond with a percentage likelihood that something is likely to happen.

3. The data are returned to the staff for aggregation. A probability curve is constructed.

4. A second questionnaire is prepared. It uses the same questions but also reports the results of the first questionnaire, showing the distribution curve of responses and noting the 25th and 75th percentiles. Respondents are reminded of their answers and asked whether they are interested in either changing their answer (particularly if they were outside the range of the 25th to 75th percentiles) or providing an anonymous paragraph or two in support of their position.

5. The results of the second round of responses are returned to staff and compiled.

6. A third questionnaire is sent to participants. It shows the data aggregated from the second cycle, contains a list of arguments submitted by participants on a particular issue, and offers the opportunity for a third vote.

7. The results of the third round are compiled and analyzed.

The experiences of Rand and other users of the Delphi Technique suggest that the degree of consensus tends to increase as the process proceeds. It's likely that people feel comfortable making what otherwise might be considered unusual arguments or positions because they can do so anonymously.

The Society of Nuclear Medicine once assembled a series of issue-oriented questions for consideration by members. In addition to asking about the likelihood that the issue would occur within a given time period, it also asked where—on a scale of +15 to –5—the individual respondent would rate the effect of that issue on the profession. (On the scale, +15 represented a windfall to the profession and –5 was a catastrophe for the profession.) Creating a scattergram of the responses enabled the society to focus its attention on those issues that were both highly likely to emerge and would have a significant influence.

The responsibility of the Council on Long-Range Planning and Development of the American Medical Association (AMA), based in Chicago, includes issuing thought-provoking reports to the AMA House of Delegates. Although the delegates do not always politically support the council's recommendations or agree with its analyses, the reports help shape their debates. The ASAE Foundation has used expert panels as part of "think tanks" it has convened on a regular basis to explore various issues. The Foundation has also supported a future focus project that uses threaded discussions over the Internet to think through major themes that associations will soon confront.

Who should serve on an expert panel? In most cases, your association's leaders will be aware of people who tend to think broadly and are future-oriented. Certainly, some of the current elected or appointed leaders should be tapped as well, provided they can take a big-picture view of the industry or profession. It's also wise to select people either on the fringes of or entirely outside the trade or profession who are known to be broad and deep thinkers.

- *Trend Analysis.* Created by the life insurance industry association, this technique depends on individual members to voluntarily read materials outside their normal range of attention—everything from *Mother Jones* on the left side of the political spectrum to *Plain Truth*, the publication of the John Birch Society, on the right. After reading the material, members file brief summaries. An association staff person reviews all the summaries and identifies any trends that appear to be working their way into more mainstream and popular media. Once identified, these trends can be deliberately researched.

- *Scenarios.* This increasingly popular technique uses scenarios or stories to generate discussion among groups of members or staff. One approach is to have the group identify several trends affecting the organization, select the two or three trends having the greatest significance, and begin asking what-if questions. For instance: What if a specific technology that's currently in the early stages of development bursts full-blown on the scene? What if the country experiences a recession? Considering various scenarios can help an organization develop the flexibility necessary to cope when changes rock its external or internal environment. ■

Related Resources

CHAPTER 1

Bethel, Sheila M. *Beyond Management to Leadership: Designing the 21st Century Association,* American Society of Association Executives Foundation, Washington, DC, 1993.

Jarratt, Jennifer, Joseph F. Coates, John B. Mahaffie, and Andy Hines. *Managing Your Future as an Association: Thinking about Trends and Working with Their Consequences 1994-2020,* American Society of Association Executives, Washington, DC, 1994.

Mack, Charles S. *The Executive's Handbook of Trade and Business Associations: How They Work and How to Make Them Work Effectively for You,* Greenwood Publishing Group Inc., New York, 1990.

Snyder, David Pearce, and Gregg Edwards. *America in the 1990s: Strategic Insights for Associations,* American Society of Association Executives, Washington, DC, 1992.

Tecker, Glenn H., and Marybeth Fidler. *Successful Association Leadership: Dimensions of 21st Century Competency for the CEO,* American Society of Association Executives, Washington, DC, 1993.

CHAPTER 2

Axelrod, Nancy R. *Creating and Renewing Advisory Boards: Strategies for Success,* National Center for Nonprofit Boards, Washington, DC, 1990.

Bloomer, John E. "Local Leadership Conferences: How to Train and Develop Local Section Leaders," *A Sharing of Expertise & Experience,* vol. 10, pp. 467-76, American Society of Association Executives, Washington, DC, 1992.

Blueprint for Board Diversity: A Cultural Diversity Resource Manual to Improve Board Effectiveness, United Way of America, Alexandria, VA, 1994.

Building an Effective Nonprofit Board: Creating a Cohesive, Knowledgeable, and Committed Governing Board, National Center for Nonprofit Boards, Washington, DC, 1994.

Cardwell, Ellen R. "The Pied Piper Principle: Attracting and Mobilizing Your Volunteers," *A Sharing of Expertise & Experience,* vol. 9, pp. 586-95, American Society of Association Executives, Washington, DC, 1991.

Carver, John. *Boards That Make a Difference: A New Design for Leadership in Non-profit and Public Organizations.* Jossey-Bass, Inc., Publishers, San Francisco, 1997.

———— and Miriam Mayhew Carver. *Reinventing Your Board: A Step-By-Step Guide to Implementing Policy Governance.* Jossey-Bass, Inc., Publishers, San Francisco, 1997.

Cober, Terilyn. "Harnessing Volunteer Efforts for Superior Performance in the Small Association," *A Sharing of Expertise & Experience,* vol. 10, pp. 565-68, American Society of Association Executives, Washington, DC, 1992.

Connor, Sharon J., Peggy Kirkwood, and Susan E. Dorn. "How to Administer a Nominating and Election Process that You Can Be Proud of," *A Sharing of Expertise & Experience,* vol. 11, pp. 194-202, American Society of Association Executives, Washington, DC, 1993.

Dorsey, Eugene C. *The Role of the Board Chairperson,* National Center for Non-profit Boards, Washington, DC, 1992.

Fadik, Becky L., and Brian Taylor. "Serving Your Association's Chapters/Sections with Field Service Representatives," *A Sharing of Expertise & Experience,* vol. 9, pp. 486-93, American Society of Association Executives, Washington, DC, 1991.

Golden, Mark J. "Involving Every Director in Association Governance," *A Sharing of Expertise & Experience,* vol. 9, pp. 162-77, American Society of Association Executives, Washington, DC, 1991.

Hartman, Charles H. "Organizational Structure Does Make a Difference," *A Sharing of Expertise & Experience,* vol. 9, pp. 17-27, American Society of Association Executives, Washington, DC, 1991.

How to Help Your Board Govern More and Manage Less, National Center for Non-profit Boards, Washington, DC, 1994.

Kilkuskie, Ann M., and Linda M. Komarow. "Energize Your Volunteers: Management Strategies That Work," *A Sharing of Expertise & Experience,* vol. 11, pp. 528-32, American Society of Association Executives, Washington, DC, 1993.

Kurtz, Daniel L. "Responsibilities of Association Directors and Officers," *A Sharing of Expertise & Experience,* vol. 11, pp. 369-76, American Society of Association Executives, Washington, DC, 1993.

Lascell, David M., and Cary M. Jensen. *Bridging the Gap Between Nonprofit and For-Profit Board Members,* National Center for Nonprofit Boards, Washington, DC, 1992.

Mathiason, Karl III. *Board Passages: Three Key Stages in a Nonprofit Board's Life Cycle,* National Center for Nonprofit Boards, Washington, DC, 1990.

McInnis, Jan. "Getting Your Volunteers to Volunteer," *A Sharing of Expertise & Experience,* vol. 13, pp. 234-39, American Society of Association Executives, Washington, DC, 1995.

Nelson, Judith Grummon. *A Guide to Building Your Board: Six Keys to Recruiting, Orienting, and Involving Nonprofit Board Members*, National Center for Nonprofit Boards, Washington, DC, 1991.

Pfau, Sandra K. "Board Membership: Is It a Power Play?" *A Sharing of Expertise & Experience*, vol. 9, pp. 44-49, American Society of Association Executives, Washington, DC, 1991.

Thornton, J. Scott. "Strategic Recruiting: Dealing with the Disappearing Volunteer Base," *A Sharing of Expertise & Experience*, vol. 10, pp. 191-200, American Society of Association Executives, Washington, DC, 1992.

CHAPTER 3

Adler, Ronald L., and Francis T. Coleman. *Employment-Labor Law Audit: Including 1996 Supplement*, Laurdan Associates, Inc., Potomac, MD, 1996.

Alvarez, Francis P., Michael Lotito, and Richard Pimentel. *The Americans with Disability Act: Making the ADA Work for You*, Society for Human Resource Management, Alexandria, VA, 1992.

Antion, Tom. "Technostress: Don't Let the Computer Chips Drive Away Your Blue Chip Staff," *A Sharing of Expertise & Experience*, vol. 12, pp. 371-76, American Society of Association Executives, Washington, DC, 1994.

Bosma, Jennifer. "Valuing Staff," *A Sharing of Expertise & Experience*, vol. 8, pp. 16-21, American Society of Association Executives, Washington, DC, 1990.

Cook, Mary F. *The AMA Handbook for Employee Recruitment and Retention*, AMACOM, New York, 1992.

A Decade of Expertise & Experience: Human Resources, American Society of Association Executives, Washington, DC, 1992.

Duffy, Kevin R. "New Hire Training and Evaluation," *A Sharing of Expertise & Experience*, vol. 11, pp. 286-93, American Society of Association Executives, Washington, DC, 1993.

Herold, Arthur L., and Gerard P. Panaro. *Employment Law Checklist*, Second Edition, Chamber of Commerce of the U.S., Washington, DC, 1994.

Jones, Bob. *How to Keep and Motivate Staff Specialists*, American Society of Association Executives, Washington, DC, 1993.

Knapp, Deirdre. "The Art and Science of Conducting Highly Effective and Legally Defensible Employment Interviews," *A Sharing of Expertise & Experience*, vol. 13, pp. 168-75, American Society of Association Executives, Washington, DC, 1995.

Lucas, Robert W. *Coaching Skills: A Guide for Supervisors*, Business One Irwin, Burr Ridge, IL, 1994.

Panaro, Gerard P. *Employment Law Manual: Recruitment, Selection, Termination*, Second Edition, Warren, Gorham & Lamont, Inc., Boston, 1993.

Performance Evaluation, American Society of Association Executives, Washington, DC, 1993.

Roderer, Phyllis J., and Sandra R. Sabo, ed. *Human Resource Management in Associations*, American Society of Association Executives, Washington, DC, 1994.

Sample Job Descriptions, American Society of Association Executives, Washington, DC, 1996.

Thiederman, Sondra. "Association Management and Diversity: Attracting, Retaining, and Motivating a Diverse Work Force," *A Sharing of Expertise & Experience*, vol. 10, pp. 182-90, American Society of Association Executives, Washington, DC, 1992.

Tracey, William R. *HR Words You Gotta Know!* AMACOM, New York, 1994.

Welcome to the World of Associations, American Society of Association Executives, Washington, DC, 1990.

Wilson, Thomas B. *Innovative Reward Systems for the Changing Workplace*, McGraw-Hill, Inc., New York, 1995.

CHAPTER 4

Axelrod, Nancy R. *Creating and Renewing Advisory Boards: Strategies for Success*, National Center for Nonprofit Boards, Washington, DC, 1990.

Bader, Barry S. *Planning Successful Board Retreats: A Guide for Board Members and Chief Executives*, National Center for Nonprofit Boards, Washington, DC, 1991.

Building an Effective Nonprofit Board: Creating a Cohesive, Knowledgeable, and Committed Governing Board, National Center for Nonprofit Boards, Washington, DC, 1994.

Carver, John. *Boards that Make a Difference*, Jossey-Bass, Inc., Publishers, San Francisco, 1997.

———. *John Carver on Board Governance*, Jossey-Bass, Inc., Publishers, San Francisco, 1993.

CEOs and Their Boards: The Art of Survival, American Society of Association Executives, Washington, DC, 1996.

Chait, Richard. *How to Help Your Board Govern More and Manage Less*, National Center for Nonprofit Boards, Washington, DC, 1993.

Dalsimer, John Paul. *Understanding Nonprofit Financial Statements*, National Center for Nonprofit Boards, Washington, DC, 1996.

Dorsey, Eugene C. *The Role of the Board Chairperson*, National Center for Nonprofit Boards, Washington, DC, 1992.

Eadie, Douglas C. *Beyond Strategic Planning: How to Involve Nonprofit Boards in Growth and Change*, National Center for Nonprofit Boards, Washington, DC, 1993.

———. *Boards That Work: A Practical Guide to Building Effective Association Boards*, American Society of Association Executives, Washington, DC, 1995.

Eadie, Douglas C., and Robert Knight. "Designing Association Boards for the 21st Century," *A Sharing of Expertise & Experience*, vol. 11, pp. 16-24, American Society of Association Executives, Washington, DC, 1993.

Effective Nonprofit Board Leadership, Applied Research and Development Institute, Denver, 1993.

Fitzpatrick, Joyce L. *The Board's Role in Public Relations and Communications*, National Center for Nonprofit Boards, Washington, DC, 1996.

Leifer, Jacqueline Covey, and Michael B. Glomb. *Legal Obligations of Nonprofit Boards*, National Center for Nonprofit Boards, Washington, DC, 1997.

Jacobs, Jerald A., and David W. Ogden. *Legal Risk Management for Associations: A Legal Compliance Training Videotape for Volunteers and Employees of Trade and Professional Associations*, 1995.

Keesey, Ray E. *Modern Parliamentary Procedure*, American Psychological Association, Washington, DC, 1994.

Lang, Andrew S. *The Financial Responsibilities of Nonprofit Boards*, National Center for Nonprofit Boards, Washington, DC, 1998.

Lascell, David M., and Cary M. Jensen. *Bridging the Gap Between Nonprofit and For-Profit Board Members*, National Center for Nonprofit Boards, Washington, DC, 1992.

Mathiason, Karl III. *Board Passages: Three Key Stages in a Nonprofit Board's Life Cycle*, National Center for Nonprofit Boards, Washington, DC, 1990.

Mueller, Robert K. *Smarter Board Meetings: For Effective Nonprofit Governance*, National Center for Nonprofit Boards, Washington, DC, 1992.

Nason, John W. *Board Assessment of the Chief Executive: A Responsibility Essential to Good Governance*, National Center for Nonprofit Boards, Washington, DC, 1990.

Nelson, Judith Grummon. *A Guide to Building Your Board: Six Keys to Recruiting, Orienting, and Involving Nonprofit Board Members*, National Center for Nonprofit Boards, Washington, DC, 1991.

Overton, George W., ed. *Guidebook for Directors of Nonprofit Corporations*, American Bar Association, Chicago, 1993.

Park, Dabney G., Jr. *Strategic Planning and the Nonprofit Board*, National Center for Nonprofit Boards, Washington, DC, 1990.

Sample Board Governance Policies, American Society of Association Executives, Washington, DC, 1998.

Slesinger, Larry H. *Self-Assessment for Nonprofit Governing Boards*, National Center for Nonprofit Boards, Washington, DC, 1991.

Szanton, Peter. *Board Assessment of the Organization: How Are We Doing?* National Center for Nonprofit Boards, Washington, DC, 1992.

Young, Dennis R., Robert M. Hollister, and Virginia A. Hodgkinson, ed. *Governing, Leading, and Managing Nonprofit Organizations*, Jossey-Bass, Inc., Publishers, San Francisco, 1993.

Zander, Alvin. *Making Boards Effective: The Dynamics of Nonprofit Governing Boards*, Jossey-Bass, Inc., Publishers, San Francisco, 1993.

CHAPTER 5

ASAE Operating Ratio Report, 11th Edition, American Society of Association Executives, Washington, DC, 2000.

Ballance, John B., and Regis J. Ebner, Jr. "Funds (Reserves) Structure as a Tool for Strategic Planning," *A Sharing of Expertise & Experience*, vol. 10, pp. 75-85, American Society of Association Executives, Washington, DC, 1992.

Cox, Ann R., and Diane James. "Compliance with the Lobbying Tax: You Can Come Out Alive; You May Even Come Out Ahead," *A Sharing of Expertise & Experience*, vol. 13, pp. 89-94, American Society of Association Executives, Washington, DC, 1995.

Dalsimer, John Paul. *Understanding Nonprofit Financial Statements*, National Center for Nonprofit Boards, Washington, DC, 1996.

A Decade of Expertise & Experience: Finance & Administration, American Society of Association Executives, Washington, DC, 1993.

Gross, Malvern J., Jr., Richard F. Larkin, and William Warshauer, Jr. *Financial & Accounting Guide for Not-for-Profit Organizations*, 6th Edition, John Wiley & Sons, Inc. New York, 2000.

Gross, Malvern J., Jr., Richard F. Larkin, Roger S. Bruttomesso, and John J. Jacobs. *Legal Risk Management for Associations: A Compliance Guide for Volunteers and Employees of Trade and Professional Associations*, American Psychological Association, Washington, DC, 1995.

Jacobs, Jerald A., and David W. Ogden. *Legal Risk Management for Associations: A Legal Compliance Training Videotape for Volunteers and Employees of Trade and Professional Associations*, 1995.

Kolar, Mary Jane, and Linda S. Huneycutt. "Doing More with Less: Getting the Most from Your Audit and Auditor," *A Sharing of Expertise & Experience*, vol. 12, pp. 56-61, American Society of Association Executives, Washington, DC, 1994.

Lang, Andrew S., and Michael Sorrells. *Completing Your IRS Form 990: A Guide for Tax-Exempt Organizations*, Revised Edition, American Society of Association Executives, Washington, DC, 1995.

McMillan, Edward J. *Budgeting and Financial Management Handbook for Not-for-Profit Organizations*, American Society of Association Executives, Washington, DC, 2000.

———. *Essential Financial Considerations for Not-for-Profit Organizations: A Guide for Nonaccounting Executives*, American Society of Association Executives, Washington, DC, 1994.

———. *Model Accounting and Financial Policies & Procedures Handbook for Not-for-Profit Organizations*, American Society of Association Executives, Washington, DC, 1999.

McNally, John J., Roger S. Bruttomesso, and Richard F. Larkin. *Financial and Accounting Guide for Not-for-Profit Organizations*, Fifth Edition, 1998 Cumulative Supplement, John Wiley & Sons, Inc. New York, 1998.

Reserve Funds and Investment Policies, American Society of Association Executives, Washington, DC, 1998.

Roady, Celia, and Howard M. Schoenfeld. "The Ten Most Common UBIT Problems for Associations," *A Sharing of Expertise & Experience*, vol. 10, pp. 96-109, American Society of Association Executives, Washington, DC, 1992.

Senft, Bruce A. "Implementing Proper Financial Controls in Your Association," *A Sharing of Expertise & Experience*, vol. 10, pp. 110-28, American Society of Association Executives, Washington, DC, 1992.

Tate, Charles F., and Joan F. Schweizer. "Complying with New Financial Statement Reporting and Accounting," *A Sharing of Expertise & Experience*, vol. 11, pp. 148-52, American Society of Association Executives, Washington, DC, 1993.

Tremper, Charles, and George Babcock. *The Nonprofit Board's Role in Reducing Risk: More Than Buying Insurance*, National Center for Nonprofit Boards, Washington, DC, 1999.

CHAPTER 6

Allen, Edith L. "How to Start Charging for Services That Used to Be Free," *A Sharing of Expertise & Experience*, vol. 11, pp. 558-63, American Society of Association Executives, Washington, DC, 1993.

Carey, Stephen C. *Marketing the Nonprofit Association*, Washington Association Research Foundation, Washington, DC, 1992.

Christian, Jack. *Marketing Designs for Nonprofit Organizations*, Fund-Raising Institute, Rockville, MD, 1992.

Graf, Kermit W. "A Practical Approach to Planning and Implementing a Successful Marketing Program," *A Sharing of Expertise & Experience*, vol. 11, pp. 383-84, American Society of Association Executives, Washington, DC, 1993.

Jans, Michael. "Get to the Heart of Your Market," *A Sharing of Expertise & Experience*, vol. 11, pp. 519-21, American Society of Association Executives, Washington, DC, 1993.

Kaufman, V. Herbert, and John E. Vowell. "Proven Techniques for Harmonizing Marketing Functions in Large Associations," *A Sharing of Expertise & Experience*, vol. 12, pp. 264-70, American Society of Association Executives, Washington, DC, 1994.

Keller, Thomas K. "Electronically Tailoring Marketing Messages to Prospects for Association Publications, Services and Membership," *A Sharing of Expertise & Experience*, vol. 9, pp. 420-28, American Society of Association Executives, Washington, DC, 1991.

Marlowe, David. "Developing and Using an Effective and Trackable Marketing Plan," *A Sharing of Expertise & Experience*, vol. 13, pp. 281-92, American Society of Association Executives, Washington, DC, 1995.

————. "Measuring the Effectiveness of Marketing Communications Strategies," *A Sharing of Expertise & Experience*, vol. 12, pp. 74-88, American Society of Association Executives, Washington, DC, 1994.

————. "Tips, Techniques and Trap Doors for Internally Driven Market Research," *A Sharing of Expertise & Experience*, vol. 12, pp. 283-99, American Society of Association Executives, Washington, DC, 1994.

Membership Satisfaction Surveys, American Society of Association Executives, Washington, DC, 1993.

Mendelsohn, Syma R. "Integrated Marketing: Raise Your Response Without Raising Your Budget," *A Sharing of Expertise & Experience*, vol. 11, pp. 390-93, American Society of Association Executives, Washington, DC, 1993.

Norris, Donald M. *Market Driven Management: Lessons Learned from 20 Successful Associations*, American Society of Association Executives Foundation, Washington, DC, 1990.

Peppers, Don, and Martha Rogers. *The One-to-One Future: Building Relationships One Customer at a Time*, Doubleday & Co., Inc., New York, 1997.

Rhinesmith, Kathleen L., and Arlene Farber Sirkin. "Maximizing the Use of Focus Groups for Associations," *A Sharing of Expertise & Experience*, vol. 10, pp. 442-51, American Society of Association Executives, Washington, DC, 1992.

Schmitt, James C. "How to Develop a Member/Customer Satisfaction Program," *A Sharing of Expertise & Experience*, vol. 12, pp. 182-86, American Society of Association Executives, Washington, DC, 1994.

Sherlock, John J., III. "Cost-Effective Marketing," *A Sharing of Expertise & Experience*, vol. 9, pp. 436-41, American Society of Association Executives, Washington, DC, 1991.

Solomon, Cathy. "Get More Satisfaction from Your Satisfaction Survey," *A Sharing of Expertise & Experience*, vol. 11, pp. 394-99, American Society of Association Executives, Washington, DC, 1993.

Stone, Bob, and John Wyman. *Successful Telemarketing*, Second Edition, NTC Business Books, Chicago, 1993.

Stone, Bob. *Successful Direct Marketing Methods*, Sixth Edition, NTC Business Books, Chicago, 1996.

Wedlock, Shireen C. "Benchmarking: Understanding Your Membership's Needs," *A Sharing of Expertise & Experience*, vol. 10, pp. 463-65, American Society of Association Executives, Washington, DC, 1992.

Wilson, Aubrey. *New Directions in Marketing: Business-to-Business Strategies for the 1990's*, William Morrow & Co., Inc. New York, 1991.

Yellen, Ira W. "Integrated Marketing and Communication for Associations," *A Sharing of Expertise & Experience*, vol. 11, pp. 400-403, American Society of Association Executives, Washington, DC, 1993.

CHAPTER 7

Association Dues, American Society of Association Executives, Washington, DC, 1999.

Brenkus, Christine M., and Thomas Wogan. "Combining Membership Renewal and Customer Service," *A Sharing of Expertise & Experience*, vol. 11, pp. 405-408, American Society of Association Executives, Washington, DC, 1993.

Burke, Christine E., and Diana McCauley. "Tackling a Three-Year Plan for Membership Development and Member Services," *A Sharing of Expertise & Experience*, vol. 9, pp. 443-53, American Society of Association Executives, Washington, DC, 1991.

Davis, William E., III. "Building a Successful Membership Recognition Program," *A Sharing of Expertise & Experience*, vol. 10, pp. 163-69, American Society of Association Executives, Washington, DC, 1992.

Delizia, James S., and Michael Kulczycki. "36 Great Ideas for Membership Marketers," *A Sharing of Expertise & Experience*, vol. 8, pp. 608-21, American Society of Association Executives, Washington, DC, 1990.

Dost, Brenda C., and Rhea L. Blanken. "Breaking the Glass Ceiling on Your Membership to Really Grow!" *A Sharing of Expertise & Experience*, vol. 12, pp. 340-45, American Society of Association Executives, Washington, DC, 1994.

Gable, Ty E. "Six Keys to Better Retention," *A Sharing of Expertise & Experience*, vol. 11, pp. 419-24, American Society of Association Executives, Washington, DC, 1993.

Griffin, Terry A. "Now That You've Got the Suppliers to Join, How Can You Retain Them?" *A Sharing of Expertise & Experience*, vol. 11, pp. 425-35, American Society of Association Executives, Washington, DC, 1993.

Hotaling, Jack R. "An Internal Association Membership Marketing Program," *A Sharing of Expertise & Experience*, vol. 8, pp. 592-97, American Society of Association Executives, Washington, DC, 1990.

Langan, John P., and Celia Roady. "Keeping Your Associate Member Dues Free from UBIT," The 9th Annual Legal Symposium, pp. 221-302, American Society of Association Executives, Washington, DC, 1995.

Mack, Charles S. "Effective Membership Process: Value Marketing to Cost Conscious Members," *A Sharing of Expertise & Experience*, vol. 8, pp. 622-28, American Society of Association Executives, Washington, DC, 1990.

Mawson, Thomas C. "Involving Your Chapters in the Marketing Function: A Case Study," *A Sharing of Expertise & Experience*, vol. 12, pp. 37-41, American Society of Association Executives, Washington, DC, 1994.

McAdoo, Richard F. "Membership Marketing: Doing More with Less," *A Sharing of Expertise & Experience*, vol. 10, pp. 453-58, American Society of Association Executives, Washington, DC, 1992.

Membership Recruitment and Retention, American Society of Association Executives, Washington, DC, 1996.

Merrill, G. Lawrence. "Enhance Member Satisfaction Through 'Fair' Dues," *A Sharing of Expertise & Experience*, vol. 11, pp. 142-47, American Society of Association Executives, Washington, DC, 1993.

Muehlbauer, Eric J. "How to Revise Your Membership Material from Recruitment to Recognition," *A Sharing of Expertise & Experience*, vol. 8, pp. 629-48, American Society of Association Executives, Washington, DC, 1990.

Peters, Ronald L., and Richard P. Whelan. "Finders Keepers or Getting a Handle on the Costs to Obtain and Keep Your Members," *A Sharing of Expertise & Experience*, vol. 12, pp. 358-65, American Society of Association Executives, Washington, DC, 1994.

Peters, Ronald L., and Richard P. Whelan. "Lifetime Value, Part II: Big Deal—How Do I Use It?" *A Sharing of Expertise & Experience*, vol. 13, pp. 240-46, American Society of Association Executives, Washington, DC, 1995.

Sente, Marjory J., and Patrick J. Scholl. "Five R's for Retaining Members," *A Sharing of Expertise & Experience*, vol. 11, pp. 446-50, American Society of Association Executives, Washington, DC, 1993.

Sirkin, Arlene Farber, and Michael P. McDermott. *Keeping Members: The Myths and Realities*, American Society of Association Executives Foundation, Washington, DC, 1995.

Thiederman, Sondra. "Capturing the Rainbow: Key Strategies for Building a Diverse Membership," *A Sharing of Expertise & Experience*, vol. 12, pp. 346-51, American Society of Association Executives, Washington, DC, 1994.

Wilson, Caryn. "Developing a Database? Don't Despair!" *A Sharing of Expertise & Experience*, vol. 9, pp. 651-60, American Society of Association Executives, Washington, DC, 1991.

Zietz, Lewis D. "Doubling Your Renewal Rate: Twenty Dynamite Techniques that Will Explode Myths About Member Renewal," *A Sharing of Expertise & Experience*, vol. 12, pp. 352-57, American Society of Association Executives, Washington, DC, 1994.

Zotta, LeAnn, ed. *500 Strategies, Tips & Ideas for Membership Professionals*, Association Advisory Council, Littleton, CO, 1994.

CHAPTER 8

Adams, John T., III. "(More Than) 25 Ways to Beat Commercial Publications in Advertising Sales," *A Sharing of Expertise & Experience*, vol. 13, pp. 48-53, American Society of Association Executives, Washington, DC, 1995.

Association Publishing Procedures Report, American Society of Association Executives, Washington, DC, 1991.

Beach, Mark, and Eric Kenly. *Getting It Printed: How to Work With Printers and Graphic Imaging Services to Assure Quality, Stay on Schedule and Control Costs*, Third Edition, North Light Books, Cincinnati, OH, 1999.

A Decade of Expertise & Experience: Communications, American Society of Association Executives, Washington, DC, 1993.

Fanson, Barbara A. *Producing a First-Class Newsletter: A Guide to Planning, Writing, Editing, Designing, Photography, Production, and Printing*, Self-Counsel Press, Bellingham, WA, 1994.

Farkas, Peter L., and Robert H. Morse. "Copyrights and Trademarks: 20 Tips for an Effective Association Policy," The 9th Annual Legal Symposium, pp. 65-105, American Society of Association Executives, Washington, DC, 1995.

Finding the Right Format, American Society of Association Executives, Washington, DC, 1990.

Graham, Anne. "Internationalizing Association Publications," *A Sharing of Expertise & Experience*, vol. 11, pp. 38-42, American Society of Association Executives, Washington, DC, 1993.

Huenefeld, John. *The Huenefeld Guide to Book Publishing*, Fifth Edition, Mills & Sanderson, Publishers, Bedford, MA, 1993.

Hunt, Scott, and Lenne P. Miller. "A Decision to Publish Model for an Association Press," *A Sharing of Expertise & Experience*, vol. 9, pp. 80-89, American Society of Association Executives, Washington, DC, 1991.

Perkins, Russell A. "Elements of Profitable Association Directory Publishing," *A Sharing of Expertise & Experience*, vol. 11, pp. 43-48, American Society of Association Executives, Washington, DC, 1993.

Publication Manual of the American Psychological Association, 4th Edition, American Psychological Association, Washington, DC, 1994.

Readership Surveys, American Society of Association Executives, Washington, DC, 1995.

Roche, William J., Jr. "How to Read and Understand Book Publishing Contracts," *A Sharing of Expertise & Experience*, vol. 9, pp. 90-97, American Society of Association Executives, Washington, DC, 1991.

Selling Advertising for Association Publications, American Society of Association Executives, Washington, DC, 1996.

Shuping, Frances, ed. *A Guide to Periodicals Publishing for Associations*, American Society of Association Executives, Washington, DC, 1995.

Smith, Ronald Ted. *Book Publishing Encyclopedia: The Secrets of Successful Publishing*, BookWorld Press, Sarasota, FL, 1994.

CHAPTER 9

Association Meeting Trends, American Society of Association Executives, Washington, DC, 1999.

Carey, Stephen C., ed. *Conducting International Meetings: A Meeting Planning and Resource Guide*, GWSAE Foundation, Washington, DC, 1993.

The Convention Liaison Council, Deloitte & Touche. *The Economic Impact of Conventions, Expositions, Meetings and Incentive Travel*, The Convention Liaison Council, Washington, DC, 1995.

Convention Liaison Council Manual: A Working Guide for Effective Meetings and Conventions, 6th Edition, Convention Liaison Council, Washington, DC, 1994.

A Decade of Expertise & Experience: Meetings & Conventions, American Society of Association Executives, Washington, DC, 1992.

A Decade of Expertise & Experience: Education, American Society of Association Executives, Washington, DC, 1992.

Jarrow, Jane E., and Ciritta B. Park. *Accessible Meetings and Conventions*, Association on Higher Education and Disability, Columbus, OH, 1992.

Kutt, Patricia, and Joseph N. Lane. "Critical Roles and Powerful Attributes of the Successful Association Educator," *A Sharing of Expertise & Experience*, vol. 8, pp. 162-66, American Society of Association Executives, Washington, DC, 1990.

LaBranche, Gary A. *Perspectives on the Future of Association Trade Shows and Exhibits*, American Society of Association Executives, Washington, DC, 1993.

McAdoo, Richard F. "Marketing Education: A Strategic Guide," *A Sharing of Expertise & Experience*, vol. 9, pp. 125-30, American Society of Association Executives, Washington, DC, 1991.

Phillips, Louis E. *The Continuing Education Guide: The CEU and Other Professional Development Criteria*, Kendall/Hunt Publishing Co., Dubuque, IA, 1994.

Planning International Meetings, American Society of Association Executives, Washington, DC, 1996.

Robertson, Susan. "Model for Continuing Education a Proven Success," *A Sharing of Expertise & Experience*, vol. 8, pp. 179-87, American Society of Association Executives, Washington, DC, 1990.

Torrence, Sara R. *How to Run Scientific and Technical Meetings*, Van Nostrand Reinhold, New York, 1991.

Voso, Michele. *The Convention and Meeting Planner's Handbook: A Step-By-Step Guide to Making Your Event a Success*, Lexington Books, Lexington, MA, 1996.

CHAPTER 10

"Codes of Ethics and Professional Standards," *The Value of Associations to American Society*, pp. 63-77, American Society of Association Executives, Washington, DC, 1990.

"Ethics in Certification: Setting Standards Consumers Can Count on," *Association Educator*, January 1992, pp. 1, 6-7, American Society of Association Executives, Washington, DC.

Balen, Samuel T., Anne Browning, Charles Johnston, Meredith A. Mullins, and Scott R. Sturzl. "Certification in a Global Marketplace," *A Sharing of Expertise & Experience*, vol. 12, pp. 2-10, American Society of Association Executives, Washington, DC, 1994.

Bosma, Jennifer, Anne Browning, and Meredith A. Mullins. "Reengineering a Mature Credentialing Program: Established Strengths and Evolutionary Vision," *Association Educator*, May/June 1994, pp. S-1 to S-4, American Society of Association Executives, Washington, DC.

Gaddy, Dale. "Certification Liability: What You Don't Know Can Hurt," *Association Educator*, November 1995, pp. 1, 4, American Society of Association Executives, Washington, DC.

Giesler, Scott D. "Thinking About Worldwide Certification?" *Association Educator*, April 1995, pp. 1, 3, 6, American Society of Association Executives, Washington, DC.

Hamm, Michael S., and Larry Allan Early. "Certification: Yes or No?" *Association Management*, December 1994, pp. 89-95, American Society of Association Executives, Washington, DC.

Hepner, Robert. "Standards That Grow Winning Chapters," *Chapter Relations*, March/April 1995, p. 5, American Society of Association Executives, Washington, DC.

Jacobs, Jerald A. *Certification & Accreditation Law Handbook*, American Society of Association Executives, Washington, DC, 1992.

Kaplan, Linda P. "The Hidden Benefits of a Certification Program," *A Sharing of Expertise & Experience*, vol. 11, pp. 10-14, American Society of Association Executives, Washington, DC, 1993.

Kelly, David M., and Kim A. Zeitlin. "Certification Marks: A Trap for the Unwary," Association Law & Policy, Oct. 15, 1994, pp. 7-8, American Society of Association Executives, Washington, DC.

Lad, Lawrence J. *Current Principles and Practices in Association Self-Regulation*, American Society of Association Executives, Washington, DC, 1992.

Owen, Deborah K. "Standard-Setting: How to Avoid Legal Hang-Ups," The 8th Annual Legal Symposium, pp. 389-408, American Society of Association Executives, Washington, DC, 1994.

Sedgwick, Grace H. "Trends in Certification: Where Are Associations Headed?" *Association Educator*, January 1996, pp. 1, 4, American Society of Association Executives, Washington, DC.

Webster, George D. "Advertising, Standardization, and Seals of Approval." *The Law of Associations*, pp. 12:1-12:77, Matthew Bender & Co., Inc. Washington, DC, 1994.

————. "Implications of Codes of Ethics," *Association Management,* December 1995, pp. 119-120, American Society of Association Executives, Washington, DC.

Webster, Hugh K. "Certification Programs: Avoiding the Legal Traps," Association Law & Policy, Oct. 15, 1995, p. 7, American Society of Association Executives, Washington, DC.

Chapter 11

Akchurin, Omar, and Deborah Smith-Cohen. "Guidelines and Insights on Establishing an Information Service," *A Sharing of Expertise & Experience,* vol. 11, pp. 546-57, American Society of Association Executives, Washington, DC, 1993.

Dignam, Monica, and Ann L. Oliveri, "Leveraging Your Research Budget," *A Sharing of Expertise & Experience,* vol. 9, pp. 413-19, American Society of Association Executives, Washington, DC, 1991.

Greenbaum, Thomas L. *The Handbook for Focus Group Research,* Revised and Expanded, Lexington Books, Lexington, MA, 1998.

Heim, Debbie, and Susan Schmidt. "Beyond Making Sense: How to Put Your Research to Work," *Association Educator,* May 1991, pp. 1, 3, 7, American Society of Association Executives, Washington, DC.

"How to Develop a Survey and Use the Results," *Membership Marketer,* February 1991, pp. 6–7, American Society of Association Executives, Washington, DC.

Lowell, William E. "How to Choose a Research Tool: The Market Is the Message," *Marketing Forum,* March/April 1995, pp. 1-2, 6, American Society of Association Executives, Washington, DC.

Rea, Louis M., and Richard A. Parker. *Designing and Conducting Survey Research: A Comprehensive Guide,* Jossey-Bass, Inc., Publishers, San Francisco, 1992.

Rhinesmith, Kathleen L., and Arlene Farber Sirkin. "Maximizing the Use of Focus Groups for Associations," *A Sharing of Expertise & Experience,* vol. 10, pp. 442-51, American Society of Association Executives, Washington, DC, 1992

Schmidt, Dale R. "Current Issues in Antitrust Law," Association Law & Policy, Nov. 1, 1995, pp. 6-7, American Society of Association Executives, Washington, DC.

"Survey of Association Surveying," *Communication News,* August 1994, pp. 1, 5, American Society of Association Executives, Washington, DC, 1994.

Webster, George D. "Statistical Reporting," *The Law of Associations,* pp. 8:1-8:22, Matthew Bender & Co., Inc. Washington, DC, 1994.

Chapter 12

"75-Plus Ways to Gain Greater Access to the ASAE Market," *Association Management,* July 1995, pp. 79-82, 84, 86, American Society of Association Executives, Washington, DC.

Clemons, Calvin K. "How to Handle Clients' Funds: Other People's Money," *AMC Connection*, Spring 1995, p. 5, American Society of Association Executives, Washington, DC.

Fernley, G. A. Taylor. "Incentive-Based Fee Arrangements: A New Spin on Management Fee Negotiations," *AMC Connection*, Summer 1995, pp. 4, 6, American Society of Association Executives, Washington, DC.

Hakanson, William P. "Survey Reveals Marketing Practices of Association Management Companies," *AMC Connection*, Spring 1995, pp. 1, 4, American Society of Association Executives, Washington, DC.

Lebovic, Mitchell E. "Formulas for Combining Your Clients' Buying Power," *AMC Connection*, Summer 1995, p. 7, American Society of Association Executives, Washington, DC, 1995.

Marketing to Associations, American Society of Association Executives, Washington, DC, 1995.

"The PRIMA Awards," *Association Management*, May 1995, pp. 99-104, American Society of Association Executives, Washington, DC.

Teagno, Gary C. *Profiting Through Association Marketing*, Business One Irwin, Homewood, IL, 1994.

CHAPTER 13

"75-Plus Ideas for Enhancing Government Relations," *Association Management*, August 1995, pp. 168-74, 176-77, 291, American Society of Association Executives, Washington, DC.

Alexander, Donald C., and Charles F. Tate. "The New Lobby Tax Law Regulations: An Association Compliance Clinic," The 9th Annual Legal Symposium, pp. 157-220, American Society of Association Executives, Washington, DC, 1995.

Allen, Mark. "How to Sell the Value of Your GR Program," *Government Relations*, September 1993, pp. 1, 4, American Society of Association Executives, Washington, DC.

Association Political Involvement (Including PACs), American Society of Association Executives, Washington, DC, 1995.

Austin, Thais. "Win Big in the Grass-Roots Political Game," *Government Relations*, October 1995, pp. 1, 4, American Society of Association Executives, Washington, DC.

Brown, Dennis. "The Chemistry of Permanent Coalitions," *Government Relations*, August 1993, pp. 3, 5, American Society of Association Executives, Washington, DC.

Cox, Ann R., and Diane James. "Compliance with the Lobbying Tax: You Can Come Out Alive; You May Even Come Out Ahead," *A Sharing of Expertise & Experience*, vol. 13, pp. 89-94, American Society of Association Executives, Washington, DC, 1995.

Cruce, Doug, and David Waymire. "Taking It to the Streets: Lobbying at Home and Under the Dome," *A Sharing of Expertise & Experience*, vol. 12, pp. 216-19, American Society of Association Executives, Washington, DC, 1994.

Dinegar, James. "Marketing Your Government Relations," *Government Relations*, November 1993, pp. 1-2, 4, 7, American Society of Association Executives, Washington, DC.

Fullilove, Morag, Mark J. Golden, and Jane Work. "Government Relations Goes High-Tech," *Association Management*, February 1995, pp. 48-50, 54, 56-59, 88, American Society of Association Executives, Washington, DC.

Fullilove, Morag. "How to Prepare for a Government Affairs Emergency," *Government Relations*, July 1993, pp. 5, 8, American Society of Association Executives, Washington, DC, 1993.

———. "Is Your Association Prepared for a Government Affairs Emergency?" *A Sharing of Expertise & Experience*, vol. 11, pp. 261-64, American Society of Association Executives, Washington, DC, 1993.

Gagen, Joe. "Successful Legislative Planning," *Government Relations*, January 1995, pp. 1, 6-8, American Society of Association Executives, Washington, DC.

Gentzel, Thomas, Dave Sheppard, and Kathy Mebus. "How PR Can Make Your Lobbying Efforts Fly," *Government Relations*, June 1995, pp. 3, 5, American Society of Association Executives, Washington, DC, 1995.

Hunt, Frederick D., Jr. "How Coalitions Work," *Association Management*, June 1993, pp. 93-94, 108, American Society of Association Executives, Washington, DC.

Kirkpatrick, Kate, ed. *Building From the Ground Up: A Government Relations Manual for Local Builders Associations*, National Association of Home Builders, Washington, DC, 1994.

Lobbying by Associations, American Society of Association Executives, Washington, DC, 1998.

Mahlmann, John J. "Maximizing the Power of Coalitions," *Association Management*, September 1995, pp. 32-39, American Society of Association Executives, Washington, DC.

Markowitz, Steven. "The State GR Pro in 1995," *Government Relations*, March 1995, pp. 1, 4-6, American Society of Association Executives, Washington, DC.

Maxwell, Bruce. *Washington Online: How to Access the Government's Electronic Bulletin Boards*, 1997, Congressional Quarterly, Inc., Washington, DC, 1997.

McCrary, Elissa. "Getting Government Affairs Information to Members," *Communication News*, June 1993, pp. 1-2, American Society of Association Executives, Washington, DC.

Nelson, E. Colette, and Michael P. O'Brien. "Taking Your Legislative Issue to Market," *Association Management*, November 1993, pp. 34-38, American Society of Association Executives, Washington, DC.

Nolan, Colleen M. "How to Be a Winner with Coalitions," *Government Relations*, July 1995, pp. 1-2, American Society of Association Executives, Washington, DC.

O'Brien, Michael P. "Stateside-Oriented GR Programs that Empower Your Chapters," *Government Relations*, July 1993, pp. 1, 3-4, 6-7, American Society of Association Executives, Washington, DC.

O'Brien, Michael P., and E. Colette Nelson. "Managing and Staffing a Government Relations Committee," *Government Relations*, September 1994, pp. 1, 4-8, American Society of Association Executives, Washington, DC.

Savio, Harry. "Building Coalitions," *Government Relations*, July 1995, pp. 3-5, American Society of Association Executives, Washington, DC.

Sharbaugh, John M. "How to Recruit and Train a Grass-Roots Army," *Government Relations*, April 1995, pp. 1, 3-4, 6, American Society of Association Executives, Washington, DC.

Smith, Michael J. "Beg, Borrow, or Steal Your Way to a Successful GR Program," *Government Relations*, January/February 1993, pp. 1-3, 6, American Society of Association Executives, Washington, DC.

Tenenbaum, Jeffrey S. "Managing Regulatory Affairs," *Government Relations*, October 1993, p. 3, American Society of Association Executives, Washington, DC,.

———. "The New Lobby Tax Rules," *Association Management*, September 1995, pp. 77-79, 88, American Society of Association Executives, Washington, DC.

"Traverse Your Government Affairs On-Line," *Government Relations*, November 1994, pp. 3, 6, American Society of Association Executives, Washington, DC.

Webster, George D. "PAC Particulars," *Association Management*, June 1995, pp. 172-73, American Society of Association Executives, Washington, DC.

Yep, Richard. "Helping Chapters with Government Relations," *Chapter Relations*, March/April 1994, p. 3, American Society of Association Executives, Washington, DC, 1994.

CHAPTER 14

"75 Successful Communication Ideas," *Association Management*, December 1995, pp. 76-78, 80-82, 84, American Society of Association Executives, Washington, DC.

Association Public Relations, American Society of Association Executives, Washington, DC, 1993.

Comeaux, Judy. "PRIMA Award Winners," *Association Management*, April, 1993, pp. 109-14, American Society of Association Executives, Washington, DC.

Cone, Carol L. "Cause-Related Marketing in the '90s," *Membership Developments*, July 1995, pp. 1-3, American Society of Association Executives, Washington, DC.

Crosson, David, and Victory Dubina. "Become the Voice of Your Industry," *Communication News*, April 1993, pp. 3-5, American Society of Association Executives, Washington, DC, 1993.

Ferguson, Sherry Devereaux. *Mastering the Public Opinion Challenge*, Irwin Professional Publishing, Burr Ridge, IL, 1993.

Fischer, Wanda A. "Annual Reports That Get Ahead," *Communication News*, June 1994, pp. 1, 3, 5, American Society of Association Executives, Washington, DC.

Kahn, Lynn D. "Coordinate What You Communicate," *Association Management*, July 1994, pp. 83-88, American Society of Association Executives, Washington, DC.

Kolakowski, Gail. "The Association Image: Building Your Identity and Influence Among Constituents," *A Sharing of Expertise & Experience*, vol. 13, pp. 278-80, American Society of Association Executives, Washington, DC, 1995.

Lee, Lorri. "75 Examples of Associations Advancing America," *Association Management*, August 1995, pp. 153-54, 156, 158-60, 162-66, 303, American Society of Association Executives, Washington, DC.

McLaughlin, Thomas A. "Lessons from United Way," *Association Management*, August 1995, pp. 24, 26, American Society of Association Executives, Washington, DC.

Pendley, Donald L. "Coaching Chapters in Public Relations," *Communication News*, July 1995, pp. 1-2, American Society of Association Executives, Washington, DC.

Quinlan, Liz W. "Launching a Public-Awareness Campaign," *Association Management*, November 1995, pp. 46-52, 90, American Society of Association Executives, Washington, DC.

Sullivan, Helen. "Launching a Public Relations Campaign," *Association Management*, February 1993, pp. 45-52, American Society of Association Executives, Washington, DC.

Tarnapol, Paula. "Focus Your Community Outreach on a Goal," *Communication News*, January 1993, pp. 1, 4, American Society of Association Executives, Washington, DC.

Wiener, Valerie. "Cost-Effective Tips: Enhancing Your Association's Public Identity," *Communication News*, February, 1995, pp. 1, 4, American Society of Association Executives, Washington, DC.

CHAPTER 15

Alessi, Russell J. "Asking for Money," *A Sharing of Expertise & Experience*, vol. 12, p. 153, American Society of Association Executives, Washington, DC, 1994.

Boyers, Karla. "The Foundation-Association Relationship: Sorting Out Boundaries and Bonds," *Association Management*, December 1994, pp. 42-52, American Society of Association Executives, Washington, DC.

Collins, Leslie A., Wilford A. Butler, and Edward K. Dorris. "101 Ideas for Successful Fund-Raising: Today and in the Future," *A Sharing of Expertise & Expe-*

rience, vol. 12, pp. 154-60, American Society of Association Executives, Washington, DC, 1994.

Fazio, Charles R. "Strategies for Fund-Raising and Program Development," *A Sharing of Expertise & Experience*, vol. 12, pp. 141-46, American Society of Association Executives, Washington, DC, 1994.

Fazio, Charles R., and Russell J. Alessi, "Strategies for Fundraising and Program Development," *A Sharing of Expertise & Experience*, vol. 11, pp. 176-81, American Society of Association Executives, Washington, DC, 1993.

Fund Raising for Associations and Association Foundations, American Society of Association Executives, Washington, DC, 1994.

"Fund-Raising Hits a New Beat," *Association Management*, April 1993, pp. 103-107, 134, 138, American Society of Association Executives, Washington, DC.

Holmes, Christine P., and William E. Lowell. "Granting Money in all the Wrong Places: A Foundation Case Study," *A Sharing of Expertise & Experience*, vol. 13, pp. 131-37, American Society of Association Executives, Washington, DC, 1995.

Hopkins, Bruce R. *Starting & Managing a Nonprofit Organization: A Legal Guide*, 3rd Edition, John Wiley & Sons, Inc., New York, 2000.

Howe, Fisher. "The Art of Raising Money," *Leadership*, pp. L45–L46, American Society of Association Executives, Washington, DC, 1993.

Kenworthy, Ann C. "Anatomy of a Capital Campaign," *Association Management*, December 1994, pp. 57-58, 60, 88, 95, American Society of Association Executives, Washington, DC.

Knappenberger, Sherry. "Keep the Fun in Fund-Raising," *Leadership*, pp. L-56–L-58, American Society of Association Executives, Washington, DC, 1995.

Nickelsberg, Barry. "Fund Raising for Associations and Their Foundations," *A Sharing of Expertise & Experience*, vol. 11, pp. 182-86, American Society of Association Executives, Washington, DC, 1993.

Quiggle, James, and Greg Munford. "Creative Funding Sources: Why Not Direct Mail?" *Communication News*, October 1993, pp. 1, 3, 5, American Society of Association Executives, Washington, DC.

Starting and Managing an Association Foundation, American Society of Association Executives, Washington, DC, 1995.

Wagner, Lilya. "Achieving Success in a Fund Raising Program," *A Sharing of Expertise & Experience*, vol. 12, pp. 135-40, American Society of Association Executives, Washington, DC, 1994.

Warwick, Mal. *How to Write Successful Fundraising Letters*, Strathmoor Press, Berkeley, CA, 1994.

Wingerter, Eugene J. "Three Fundamental Questions Before Starting a Foundation," *A Sharing of Expertise & Experience*, vol. 12, pp. 151-52, American Society of Association Executives, Washington, DC, 1994.

Chapter 16

"CEO to CEO: Strategic Planning Time Lines," *Association Management*, February 1996, p. 183, American Society of Association Executives, Washington, DC, 1996.

Downs, Phillip E., Bryan E. Silbermann, and Nancy J. Tucker. "Implications of Integrating MIS and Strategic Planning," *A Sharing of Expertise & Experience*, vol. 13, pp. 293-96, American Society of Association Executives, Washington, DC, 1995.

Eadie, Douglas C. *Beyond Strategic Planning: How to Involve Nonprofit Boards in Growth and Change*, National Center for Nonprofit Boards, Washington, DC, 1993.

Kaufman, Richard, and Michael T. Pfeiffer. "Re-Energizing Your Entire Association Through Integrated Strategic Thinking," *A Sharing of Expertise & Experience*, vol. 13, pp. 8-13, American Society of Association Executives, Washington, DC, 1995.

Leopold, Bea, and Janet Unger. "If It Ain't Broke, Fix It: Strategic Planning from a Position of Strength," *A Sharing of Expertise & Experience*, vol. 11, pp. 533-38, American Society of Association Executives, Washington, DC, 1993.

Long-Range Planning, American Society of Association Executives, Washington, DC, 1995.

Murphy, John M. "National/Chapter Strategic Partnering: A Four-Question Model for Planning Success," *A Sharing of Expertise & Experience*, vol. 11, pp. 458-62, American Society of Association Executives, Washington, DC, 1993.

———. "National/Chapter Strategic Partnering: A Four-Question Model for Planning Success," *Chapter Relations*, November/December 1995, pp. 1, 4, American Society of Association Executives, Washington, DC.

Perlov, Dadie. "The Strategic Plan," *Leadership*, pp. L-69-L-72; L-77, American Society of Association Executives, Washington, DC, 1995.

Reynolds, Jon, and Billie P. Spellman. "Enhance Your Strategic Plan with Member Input," *Membership Developments*, December 1995, p. 3, American Society of Association Executives, Washington, DC.

Rogers, Thomas, and James Alvino. "The Strategic Action Management Model (SAMM): Getting Your Association Back on Track," *A Sharing of Expertise & Experience*, vol. 11, pp. 239-45, American Society of Association Executives, Washington, DC, 1993.

Whitney, Ken. "Building Commitment into Strategic Plan," *Association Management*, September 1994, pp. 61-66, American Society of Association Executives, Washington, DC.

Chapter 17

Blanken, Rhea L. and Allen Liff. *Embracing the Future: An Action Guide for Association Leaders*, American Society of Association Executives, Washington, DC, 1999.

Coates, Joseph F. *Issues Identification and Management: The State of the Art of Methods and Techniques*, Electric Power Institute, 1985.

Facing the Future: A Report on the Major Trends and Issues Affecting Associations, American Society of Association Executives Foundation, Washington, DC, 1999.

Hamel, Gary and C. K. Pralahad. *Competing for the Future.* Harvard Business School Publishing, Cambridge, MA, 1996.

Jarrett, Jennifer, Joseph F. Coates, John B. Mahaffie, and Andy Hines. *Managing Your Future as an Association: Thinking About Trends and Working With Their Consequences 1994-2020*, American Society of Association Executives, Washington, DC, 1994.

Tecker, Glenn, and Marybeth Fidler. *Successful Association Leadership: Dimensions of 21st-Century Competency for the CEO*, American Society of Association Executives, Washington, DC, 1993.

Index

A

ABA Journal, 67
Academia Secretorum Naturae of Naples, 5
Accounting software, 40
Accounting system, 39
Accreditation, 81, 84–86
Ad hoc committees, 21, 32–33
Advertising:
  public policy, 104
  supplier, 92, 93, 95
Agenda for meetings, 21–23
  suggested, 22–23
  supporting materials for, 23
  traditional model for, 21–22
Allegiance for Associations, 57
Almond Board of California, 7
Aluminum Association, 93
American Academy of Arts and Sciences (AAAS), 5
American Academy of Family Physicians (AAFP), 68
American Animal Hospital Association (AAHA), 33
American Association of Fund Raising Counsel, 90
American Association of Museums (AAM), 107
American Association of Retired Persons (AARP), 59, 65
American Bar Association of Chicago, 67
American College of Radiology, 26
American Czech & Slovak Association, 15
American League of Lobbyists, 14
American Library Association (ALA), 68
American Medical Association, 6
  Council on Long-Range Planning and Development, 134
American National Standards Institute (ANSI), 83
American Nurses Association, 15, 62
American Philosophical Society, 5
American Psychiatric Association, 5–6
American Recreation Coalition, 104
American Society for Testing and Materials (ASTM), 83

American Society of Association Executives (ASAE), 82
  compensation surveys, 28
  foundation, 18, 119, 134
  history of, 5
  Operating Ratio Report, 45, 48, 55, 69
  requests for information, 49
  statistics, 7
American Standard Code for Information Interchange (ASCII), 82
American Statistical Association, 5
Americans with Disabilities Act, 10, 77
American Trade Association Executives, 5
American Trucking Association, 26
Amicus curiae briefs, 105
Annual meetings, 73–74
  see also Meetings
Art Directors Club of Metropolitan Washington (ADCMW), 85
Association Executive Compensation & Benefits Study (ASAE), 28
Association management companies, 26
Association Meeting Trends, 73
Association of American Railroads, 5
Association Publishing Procedures, 69
Associations:
  budgeting, *see* Budgeting
  businesses compared to, 8–10
  classification of, 7–8
  financial management, *see* Budgeting; Financial statements; Investments
  foundations, *see* Foundations
  governance of, *see* Governance structures
  government relations, *see* Government relations
  history of, 3–6
  marketing by, *see* Marketing
  meetings, *see* Meetings
  membership issues, *see* Membership
  number of, 2, 3
  professional, *see* Professional societies
  public relations, *see* Public relations
  publishing by, *see* Publications
  research by, *see* Research and statistics
  size of, 8–9
  staff, *see* Staff

standard-setting by, *see* Standards
strategic planning by, *see* Strategic planning
suppliers, *see* Suppliers
trade, *see* Trade associations
unique nature of, 2
volunteers, *see* Volunteers
Audioconferences, 77
Audiotapes, 69, 77
Audited financial statement, 45
Automotive Trade Association of the
Greater Washington (D.C.) Area,
74

B

Baby Boomers, 30, 31, 32, 36, 37
Balance sheet, 44
Baruch, Bernard, 4–5
Benchmarking studies, 90
Board of directors, 13
acting as a unit, 19–20
agenda for meetings, 21–23
suggested, 22–23
supporting materials for, 23
traditional model for, 21–22
associate members, seats for, 98
with at-large members, 14
chief staff executive, relationship with,
16–18, 19–20
-committee relationship, 16, 20
division of authority between staff and,
18–19
electronic meetings of, 77
of foundations, 96, 117–18
key roles of, 19–20
selection and election of, 23
size of, 13
structural options, 13–15
suppliers as members of, 98
Boards That Make a Difference (Carver),
19–20
Book Links, 68
Books, associations publishing, 65
Broadcast fax, 52, 69, 103, 107
Budget and finance committee, 42–43
Budgeting, 38–43, 52
assumptions, 40–42
expenses, 40, 41, 42
functional budgets, 40, 52

historical data, 42
preparation of budgets, 40
program budgets, 40
revenues, 42, 43
roles of staff and volunteers in, 42–43
unrelated business income, 40
Building Owners and Managers
Association (BOMA), 10
Businesses, comparison of associations
with, 8–10
Business plan, 53
Bylaws, 13, 20

C

California Dental Association, 82, 103
California Dental Association Foundation,
91
Carver, John, 19–20
Cash flow statement, 45
Cash position, 44
Catering at meetings, 76
CD-ROMs, 69, 77
Center for Substance Abuse Prevention
(CSAP), 112
Certification, 81, 83–84, 85–86
Chamber of Commerce of the State of
New York, 4
Chapters:
conflicts between national organization
and, 16
as recruitment tool, 61–62
staffing by, 26
Charitable organizations, 117
board of directors of, 14, 18
distinguished from associations, 7
foundations, *see* Foundations
under IRS Code, 7, 16, 91, 102, 117, 118
lobbying by, rules regulating, 102
Chart of accounts, 43
Chief staff executive, 12
accountability of staff to, 28
balance of power between board of
directors and, 16–18, 19–20
chart of accounts and, 43
culture of association and, 24, 29
hiring of, 19
Cigarette Manufacturers Association
(CMA), 113
Clancy, Tom, 10

Classifieds, 69
Clinton, Bill, 128
Coalitions among associations to address
    public policy issues, 104
Codes of ethics, 81–82
COMDEX, 94
Commitment, fostering, 33–34
Committees:
    ad hoc, 21, 32–33
    agenda for meetings and, 21–23
    board-appointed, 20
    budgeting process and, 42–43
    categories of, 22
    electronic meetings of, 77
    recommendations to the board, 20
    relationship between boards of direc-
        tors and, 16, 20
    staff-appointed, 20
    standing, 20–21, 32, 33
    trade show advisory, 94–95
Compensation:
    of staff, 28–29
    surveys, 90
Computer-to-plate (CTP) technology, 69
Congress, 105
Congressional testimony, 104
Contacts, making, see Networking
Conventions, 73–74
Cooperative associations, 48
Corporate membership organizations,
    recruitment efforts by, 59, 61
Corporate View: How Business Executives
    Rate Their Trade Associations, The,
    57, 60
Council for Advancement and Support of
    Education (CASE), 69
Council of Machine Tool and Equipment
    Services, 5
Courtesy bias, 50
Crises, public relations during, 113–15
Critical Competencies of Association
    Executives (Lawrence Leiter &
    Company), 38
Culture of the association, 24, 29

D

Dairy Council, Inc., 111
Delphi technique, 133
Demographic analysis, 132

Design standards, 82
Direct mail, 52, 59, 116, 118
Discrimination in hiring, 27
Distribution methods, information, 53
Dues, 9, 55–58
    allocated to lobbying, 102
    based on goods and services provided,
        56–58
    based on size, volume, or wealth, 54,
        55–56
    flat- or fixed-rate, 54, 55
    for foreign members, 60
    multiple types of memberships and, 56
    organizational politics and, 56
    publications as part of, 67
    from suppliers, 56, 93, 98
Dunlop, John, 18

E

Economic indicators, industry research
    used as, 90
Editorial control of association publica-
    tions, 67
Educational meetings, 74, 77–78
    see also Meetings
Election of board of directors, 23
Electronic Industries Association, 94
Electronic meetings, 73, 77–78
e-mail:
    newsletters, 66
    promotion through, 52
Employees, see Staff
Endorsed programs, 96
Envelope Manufacturers Association of
    America, 14–15, 61
Executive Compensation Service, 28
Exhibit fees, 92, 93
Expenses:
    budgeting for, 40, 41, 42
    see also Financial statements
Expert panels, 133–34
Expositions/trade shows, 74, 78

F

Face-to-face interviews as marketing
    research tool, 50
Family Practice Management, 68
Fax-on-demand publications, 69

Federal grants for research, 91
Federal Trade Commission, 81
Federations:
    governance of, 14
    membership of, 2, 7–8, 62
Financial Accounting Standards Board, 82
Financial management, *see* Budgeting;
        Financial statements; Investments
Financial statements, 38, 39
    audited statement, 45
    balance sheet, 44
    cash flow statement, 45
    chart of accounts, 43
    income and expense statement, 44
Fire Protection Code, 82
Flex-time, 29
Focus groups as marketing research tool,
        51
Food and Drug Administration, 113
Food Institute, 89
Food Retailing Review, 89
Foundation of the American Society of
        Association Executive, 18, 119,
        134
Foundations, 116–20
    charitable activities and, 117
    fund-raising by, 116, 117, 118–20
    operational issues, 117–18
    relationship to its parent association,
        118
    research funded by, 91
    supplier contributions to, 97
    termination provisions, 118
Four Ps of marketing, 51–53
Franklin, Benjamin, 5
Fraternal organizations, 6
Freelance writers, 67
Functional budgets, 40, 52
Funding of research, 91
Fund-raising by foundations, 116, 117,
        118–20

G

Generally Accepted Accounting Principles
        (GAAP), 82
Gen-Xers, 30, 31, 32, 36, 37
Gifts to foundations, 116, 119–20
"Golden handcuff," 34, 58
Governance committees, 22

Governance structures, 9, 12–23
    board of directors and, *see* Board of
        directors
    bylaws, 13, 20
    committees, *see* Committees
    conflict, potential areas of, 15–18
        board-staff relationships, 16–18
        chapters, 16
        committees, 16
        special interest groups, 15–16
    division of authority between staff and
        board, 18–19
    for foundations, 117–18
    meetings and, 73
        agenda for, *see* Agenda for
            meetings
    structural options for, 13–15
Government relations, 100–107,
        103–104
    advocacy activities, 103–104
    agreeing on the organization's stance on
        issues, 103
    branches of the government and,
        104–105
    coalitions of associations, 104
    collection and dissemination of infor-
        mation about emerging issues,
        102–103
    lobbying, 16, 40, 101–102, 103–104,
        105
        dues allocated to, 102
    political action committees (PACs),
        100, 103, 105–106
Guilds, 3–4

H

Health Insurance Agency of American
        (HIAA), 56
Herzberg, Frederick, 34
"Hierarchy of needs," 34
Hill, The, 104, 111
Hiring:
    of chief staff executive, 19
    of staff:
        discriminatory practices, 27
        growth of association and, 25–26
History of associations, 3–6
Hotels, holding meetings at, 76
House of delegates, 13, 14

How to Keep and Motivate Staff Specialists (Jones), 27, 28
Hunt for Red October, The (Clancy), 10

I

Income and expense statement, 44
Individual membership organizations, recruitment efforts by, 59, 61
Information:
    delivery systems for, 53
    as membership benefit, 57
    as product of associations, 51–52
    publishing of, *see* Publications
    see also Research and statistics
Institute of Internal Auditors, 66
Internal Auditor, 66
Internal Revenue Service (IRS), 43, 117
    advertising sales and, 95
    classifications for not-for-profit organizations:
        501(c)(3) status (charitable organization), 7, 16, 91, 102, 117, 118
        501(c)(4) status (social welfare organizations), 7
        501(c)(5) status (charitable organization), 98
        501(c)(6) status, 7, 16, 91, 117
    sponsorships and, 96
    supplier-association relationships and, 97–99
    supplier dues and, 56, 98
    unrelated business income, *see* Unrelated business income
International Association of Amusement Parks and Attractions (IAAPA), 60–61
International Association of Exposition Management, 94
International Fabricare Institute, 111
International members, 59, 60
International Standards Organization (ISO), 83
Internet, 52, 78, 103–104, 134
    electronic meetings on the, 77
    volunteers' use of, 37
    Web sites, association, *see* Web sites
Interviews as marketing research tool, 50–51
Investments, 45

Issues management, 102–103

J

Job sharing, 29
Joint Commission for the Accreditation of Healthcare Organizations, 84, 85
Jones, Bob, 27, 28
Journals:
    scientific, 66
    see also Publications
Judicial branch of the government, dealings with, 105

K

Kellogg Foundation, 91
Key-contact programs, 103

L

Labor unions, 98, 105
Lawrence Leiter & Company, 38
Leadership development, 30, 34
Leading the Association: Striking the Right Balance Between Staff and Volunteers (Dunlop), 18
Legislation, monitoring and lobbying for, *see* Government relations
Licensure, 83
Listservers, 37, 70, 77, 103
Lobbying, 16, 40, 101–102, 103–104, 105
    dues allocated to, 102
Local and regional associations, number of, 2, 7
Local governments, relations with, 105
Logistics for meetings, 75–77

M

Magazines, *see* Publications
Mailing list rental, 96–97
Management reports, *see* Financial statements
Marketing, 46–53
    basis of, 47
    defining markets, 9, 10, 47–48
    the Four Ps of, 51–53
    market research, 48–53, 90
    market segmentation, 48
    meeting content determined by, 74

promotional activities, 6–7, 47, 52
Maslow, Abraham, 34
Meeting Professional International (MPI),
　93
Meetings, 6, 72–79
　agenda for, *see* Agenda for meetings
　determining content of, 74–75
　electronic, 73, 77–78
　logistics, 75–77
　presenters of information at, 74
　revenues from, 73
　site selection, 76, 77
　traditional, 73–74
　venues, 37, 76, 77
　volunteer concerns about, 37
Membership, 2, 54–63
　"associate" or "affiliate," 93, 97, 98
　benefits, 54, 57–58
　corporate membership organizations,
　　59, 61
　data-based value tracking, 57, 58
　dues, *see* Dues
　of federations, 2, 7–8, 62
　finding out what members want from,
　　54
　growth opportunities, 59–60
　individual membership organizations,
　　59, 61
　organizational considerations, 60–62
　recruitment, 58–59, 61–62
　retention of, 58
　vertically integrated, 92, 93
Mining of data, 48
Mintzberg, Henry, 129
Mission, 9
　board of directors' role in defining the,
　　19
　statement, 124–25, 126, 128
Monitoring role of board of directors, 20
Mosedale, Susan, 60, 61
Motivation:
　of staff members, 29
　theories of, 34–35
Museum Advocacy Team (MAT), 107
Museums and federal tax legislation,
　106–107

N

Name changes, 59, 60

National Association of Amusement Parks,
　60
National Association of Home Builders, 89
National Association of Purchasing
　Managers, 90
National Association of REALTORS®
　(NAR), 59
National Association of Schools of Public
　Administration, 84
National associations:
　chapters of, *see* Chapters
　classification of, 7–8
　number of, 2, 3, 7
National Beer Wholesalers Association
　(NBWA), 112
National Council of Health Certifying
　Agencies (NCHCA), 83
National Electrical Manufacturers
　Association, 48
National Federation of Independent
　Businesses (NFIB), 33, 52
National Fire Protection Association, 82,
　83
National Geographic Society, 65
National Industrial Conference Board, 4
National Journal, 104
National Manufacturing Week, 94
National Organization for Competency
　Assurance (NOCA), 83
National Recovery Administration, 5
National Retail Hardware Association
　(NRHA), 70
Networking, 60, 78, 131–32
　as membership benefit, 57
　volunteering as means of, 35
Networking committees, 22
Newsletters, *see* Publications
New York Hospitality and Tourism
　Association, 59
New York Hotel/Motel Association, 59
New York Stock Exchange, 4
North American Free Trade Association
　(NAFTA), 70

O

Omnibus Budget Reconciliation Act of
　1993, 107
Omnibus trade show, 94
Ontario Chiropractic Association, 34

Operating Ratio Report (ASAE), 45, 48, 55, 69, 101
Operating ratios, 44
Operation ratios, 90
Organizational chart, flattening of, 26
Orientation program, 27–28, 36
Outsourcing, 26, 68, 77

P

Packaging Machinery Manufacturers Institute, 93–94
Pack Expo, 93–94
Part-time staff, 25
Pecan Growers Board, 6–7
Performance standards, 82
Periodicals, *see* Publications
Pharmaceutical Manufacturers Association (PMA), 128
Pharmaceutical Research and Manufacturers of America (PhRMA), 128
Planning, *see* Strategic planning
Policies & Procedures in Association Management, 26, 55, 57, 81, 89, 93, 101, 105, 115, 117
Policy committees, 22
Policy setting, board of directors' role in, 19
Political action committees (PACs), 100, 103, 105–106
Pork Producers Council, 48, 111
Price:
    information of past pricing, 4
    setting prices on products and services, 52
Printing of publications, 69
Production of publications, 68–69
Product of associations, 51–52
Productos Nuevos, 70
Professional societies:
    budgeting, *see* Budgeting
    categories of, 6
    financial management, *see* Budgeting; Financial statements; Investments
    foundations, *see* Foundations
    governance, *see* Governance
    government relations, *see* Government relations
    history of, 5–6

marketing by, *see* Marketing
meetings, *see* Meetings
membership issues, *see* Membership
membership of, 2
public relations, *see* Public relations
publishing by, *see* Publications
research by, *see* Research and statistics
staff, *see* Staff
standard-setting by, *see* Standards
strategic planning by, *see* Strategic planning
suppliers, *see* Suppliers
volunteers, *see* Volunteers
Program budgets, 40
Program committees, 22
Promotional activities, 6–7, 47, 52
Publications, 64–70
    advertising by suppliers in, 95
    contributors of content, 66–67
    "controlled circulation" of, 67
    delivery methods, 69–70
    editorial control, 67
    "house organs," 67
    as part of dues, 67
    production issues, 68–69
    types of periodicals, 65–66
Public policy advertising, 104
Public policy issues, legislative representation on, *see* Government relations
Public relations, 108–15
    in crisis situations, 113–15
    key audiences, 110–12
        customers of members, 111
        general public, 112
        government regulators and legislators, 111–12
        the media, 112
        members, 110–11
    targeting of campaigns, 109
Publishing software packages, 68

Q

Questionnaires, marketing research using, 49–50

R

Radiological Society of North America, 94
Rand Corporation, 133

Random sampling, 49–50
Recognition of volunteers, 36
Recruitment:
    membership, 58–59, 61–62
    of volunteers, 31–32
Regional and local associations, number
    of, 2, 7
Registration compared to certification,
    83–84
Regulation of an industry or professional,
    see Standards
Regulatory agencies, 105, 111
Research and statistics, 88–91
    factors to consider, 90–91
    funding sources for, 91
    market, 48–51, 90
    parties conducting, 90
    scope and variety of available, 89
    types of studies, 89–90
    used to improve image of trade or pro-
        fession, 88, 90
    validity and usefulness of, 91
Revenues, 48, 67, 73
    budgeting process and, 42, 43
    from dues, *see* Dues
    see also Financial statements
Rise and Fall of Strategic Planning, The
    (Mintzberg), 129
Roberts' Rules of Order, 22
Roll Call, 104, 111
Royalties, 96

S

Safety standards, 82
Scenarios, 134
Scientific journals, 66
Scientific societies, 5, 6
    presentations at meetings of, 75
Sherman Antitrust Act, 4, 81
Sierra Club, 104
Society of Nuclear Medicine, 59, 75, 104,
    134
Special interest groups within associations,
    15–16
    publications geared to, 66
Sponsorships, 92, 93, 95–96
Staff, 24–29
    accountability to chief staff executive,
        28

average staff size, 25
budgeting expenses for, 40
budgeting process, role in, 42
chief staff executive, *see* Chief staff
    executive
communications among, 24, 26, 29
compensation of, 28–29
governance structure and, *see*
    Governance structures
motivation of, 29
number of people employed by associa-
    tions, 7
organizational chart, flattening of, 26
part-time, 25
responding to growth of association,
    25–26
-volunteer relationship, 28, 36
writing of publication articles by, 66–67
Staff specialists, 24, 26–28, 47
Standard Rate and Data Service (SRDS),
    95
Standards:
    accreditation, 81, 84–86
    certification, 81, 83–84, 85–86
    codes of ethics, 81–82
    input and outcome measurements and,
        85–86
    technical, 82–83
Standing committees, 20–21, 32, 33
State associations, number of, 2, 7
State governments, relations with, 105
Statistics on an industry or profession,
    research to gather, *see* Research
    and statistics
Strategic planning, 122–29
    benefits of, 123–24
    elements of good, 128–29
    steps in, 124–28
    trends forecasting, 130–34
Subsidiaries, for-profit:
    purposes of, 10
Suppliers, 48, 116
    advertising, 92, 93, 95
    divergent interests of core members
        and, 91, 98–99
    dues from, 56, 93, 98
    endorsed programs and royalties, 96
    exhibit fees, 92, 93
    foundation contributions from, 97
    mailing list rental, 96–97

as a market, 92–98
sponsorships, 92, 93, 95–96
trade shows, 93
Supreme Court, U.S., 4
Surveys, marketing, 49–50

T

Taxation:
of foundations, 120
legislation, 106–107
unrelated business income, 40, 95,
97–98
see also Internal Revenue Service (IRS)
Tax Reform Act of 1986, 106–107
Technical standards, 82–83
Telecommuting, 29
Teleconferencing, 37, 77
Telephone interviews as marketing
research tool, 50
Telephone marketing, 52
Television networks, public policy advertising on, 104
Tobacco industry, 113
Trade associations:
budgeting, *see* Budgeting
financial management, *see* Budgeting;
Financial statements; Investments
foundations, *see* Foundations
governance of, *see* Governance
government relations, *see* Government
relations
history of, 3–5
marketing by, *see* Marketing
meetings, *see* Meetings
membership issues, *see* Membership
membership of, 2
public relations, *see* Public relations
publishing by, *see* Publications
research by, *see* Research and statistics
staff, *see* Staff
standard-setting by, *see* Standard
strategic planning by, *see* Strategic planning
suppliers, *see* Suppliers
volunteers, *see* Volunteers
Trade show advisory committee, 94–95
Trade shows/expositions, 74, 78, 93–95
virtual, 95
Training:

over the Internet, 78
of volunteers, 36
Trends forecasting, 130–34

U

Unique nature of associations, 2
U.S. Department of Commerce, 4, 133
U.S. Department of Labor, 133
U.S. Justice Department, 81
U.S. Naval Institute, 10
United Way of America, 8
Unrelated business income, 40, 95, 97–98
Unruh, Jesse, 105

V

Value-based pricing, 52
*Verdict: Professionals Evaluate Their
Individual Membership Societies,
The*, 57, 60
Videotapes, 69, 77
Volunteers, 30–37
budgeting process, role in, 42–43
clarifying the commitment necessary
for, 35–37
committees, *see* Committees
expectations of, 30, 35
importance of, 32–34
leadership development from, 30, 34
reasons for involvement, 35
recognition of, 36
recruitment of, 31–32
-staff relationship, 28, 36
training of, 36
writing of publication articles by, 66

W

Wall Street Journal, 90
Washington Post, 104, 111, 113
Web sites, 103
advertising, 95
association information available on,
69–70
support for group decision making on,
77
World Council, 60, 61
World Future Society, 65
World War II, 5

About ASAE Publications

The American Society of Association Executives in Washington, DC, is an individual membership organization made up of more than 25,000 association executives and suppliers. Its members manage leading trade associations, individual membership societies, and voluntary organizations across the United States and in 44 countries around the globe. It also represents suppliers of products and services to the association community.

This book is one of the hundreds of titles available through the ASAE Bookstore. ASAE publications keep you a step ahead by providing you and your staff with valuable information resources for executive management, finance, human resources, membership, career management, fundraising, and technology.

A complete catalog of titles is available on the ASAE Web site at **www.asaenet.org** or call the Member Service Center at (202) 371-0940 for the latest printed catalog.

www.asaenet.org

Related Resources from ASAE

To order ASAE publications, visit the online bookstore at
www.asaenet.org/bookstore or contact the ASAE Member Service
Center by phone (202) 371-0940 or fax (202) 371-8315.

Model Accounting and Financial Policies & Procedures Handbook for Not-for-Profit Organizations
By Edward J. McMillan, CPA, CAE

An essential resource for the executive responsible for creating board-approved financial and accounting policies and procedures. Streamline this process with more than 100 sample forms and policies that may be customized to fit your organization's needs. The forms and policies are included in the book and on CD-ROM. Major topics include internal financial statement formats, a new chart of accounts, and an accounting and financial policies and procedures manual.

1999 • 150 pages • softcover and CD-ROM • ISBN 0-88034-157-2
Product # LST-216712

Budgeting and Financial Management Handbook for Not-for-Profit Organizations
By Edward J. McMillan, CPA, CAE

McMillan's "Continuous Budgeting" and financial management program breaks time-consuming annual budgeting into twelve monthly steps that are easy to implement and monitor. Also included in this bestseller are sample forms and financial statements, formats for sending budget documents to your approving body, and methods for addressing budget problems.

2000 • 128 pages • softcover • ISBN 0-88034-158-0
Product # LST-216722

Essential Accounting, Tax, and Reporting Requirements for Not-for-Profit Organizations
By Edward J. McMillan, CPA, CAE

The accounting principles, tax issues, and reporting requirements of not-for-profit organizations are remarkably different from those affecting commercial organizations. This book is a valuable tool for bookkeepers, managers, volunteers, and auditing CPA firms who work for not-for-profit organizations. Includes complete explanations of the four standards for not-for-profit organizations: Statement of Financial Accounting Standards #116, #117, #124, and #136.

2000 • 100 pages • softcover • ISBN 0-88034-159-9
Product # LST-216721

HUNDREDS OF BOOKS ONLINE
www.asaenet.org/bookstore

Related Resources from ASAE

To order ASAE publications, visit the online bookstore at
www.asaenet.org/bookstore or contact the ASAE Member Service
Center by phone (202) 371-0940 or fax (202) 371-8315.

Allegiance: Fulfilling the Promise of One-to-One Marketing for Associations
By Dale G. Paulson

Why do members write you a check? The number of reasons is surprisingly limited, and by using the Allegiance program you'll capture a code for each member that will form the basis of your relationship. The system is easy to implement and requires no special software programs or elaborate mathematical formulas.

1998 • 78 pages • softcover • ISBN 0-88034-139-4
Product # LST-216790

Associations and the Global Marketplace: Profiles of Success
By Kimberly Svevo-Cianci

Learn how to expand memberships internationally, reach broader markets for conferences and trade shows, increase participation through affiliates and chapters, sell publication subscriptions worldwide, and reach additional users of networked databases and global information services. Each of the case studies tells of an association's experience in meeting the challenges of entering the global marketplace.

1995 • 353 pages • softcover • ISBN 0-88034-092-4
Product # LST-216525

Association Dues
ASAE Background Kit

A solid overview of planning, setting, and managing membership dues as a primary source of association income. Topics include dues structures, accounting for dues income, legal and tax issues, and handling a dues increase. Supplemented with sample documents and benchmarking statistics.

1999 • 144 pages • spiralbound
Product # LST-121015

Other Books from ASAE

To order ASAE publications, visit the online bookstore at
www.asaenet.org/bookstore or contact the ASAE Member Service
Center by phone (202) 371-0940 or fax (202) 371-8315.

Millennium Membership:
How to Attract and Keep Members in the New Marketplace
By Mark Levin, CAE

The needs and expectations of your members are changing
fast. *Millennium Membership* guides you through the steps you
must take to attract and keep members. Topics include invest-
ing in technology, branding, and moving from mass marketing
to mass customization.

2000 • 154 pages • softcover • ISBN 0-88034-163-7
Product # LST-216812

Keeping Members: The Myths and Realities
By Arlene Farber Sirkin and Michael McDermott

Are you recruiting for retention or just one year? *Keeping
Members* redefines membership as the core business for associations and other nonprofit organizations. The authors dispel
12 popular myths about retention and reveal key strategies for
growth, focusing on how CEOs, staff, and volunteers each have
key roles to play in recruiting and keeping members.

1995 • ASAE Foundation • 125 pages • softcover • ISBN 0-88034-099-01
Product #: LST-213551

The National-Chapter Partnership:
A Guide for the Chapter Relations Professional
Edited by James DeLizia

Written for and by chapter relations professionals, this guide
will help you strengthen your national-chapter partnerships.
Each chapter includes a self-assessment for building your
chapter relations program. Ideas are generously illustrated
with samples from other associations. Contents include: The Organization of
Association Chapters. Legal and Tax Considerations. Empowering Chapters
Through Effective Communications. Membership Development. Implementing Government Relations Programs at the Chapter Level. Developing New
Chapters. The Chapter Relations Professional.

1993 • 335 pages • spiralbound • ISBN 0-88034-058-4
Product #: LST-217172

HUNDREDS OF BOOKS ONLINE
www.asaenet.org/bookstore